센치한 Listening 길들이기

감성 맞춤 내신 공략

도약 **2**

센치한 LISTENING 길들이기 도약 2

출판일 | 1판 1쇄 발행 2014년 8월 29일

지은이 | 손가람, Brantley Smith
펴낸이 | 최회영
책임편집 | 김소연, 이수미
영문교열 | 이윤선, 윤은지, 강소영, Peggy Anderson
디자인 | 성윤지, 노영남, 이보람
펴낸곳 | (주)컴퍼스미디어
출판신고 | 1980년 3월 29일 제 406-2007-00046 © ㈜ 웅진씽크빅 2011
주소 | 서울특별시 서초구 서초2동 1360-31 정진빌딩 3층
전화 | (02)3471- 0096
홈페이지 | http://www.compasspub.com
ISBN | 978-89-6697-781-9

01

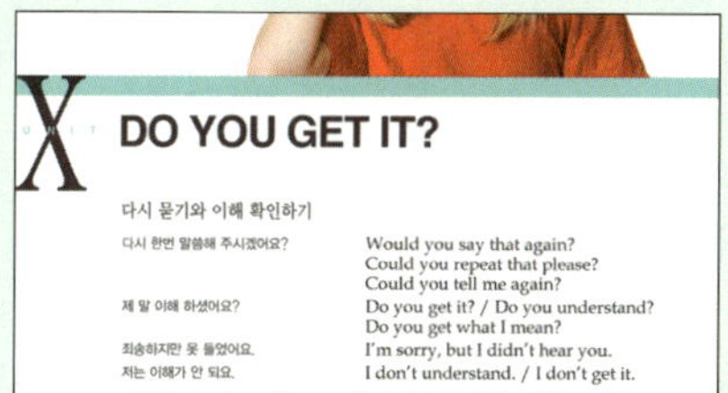

Introduction

Unit에서 학습의 초점이 되는 주요 의사소통 기능과 예문들을 학습합니다.

02

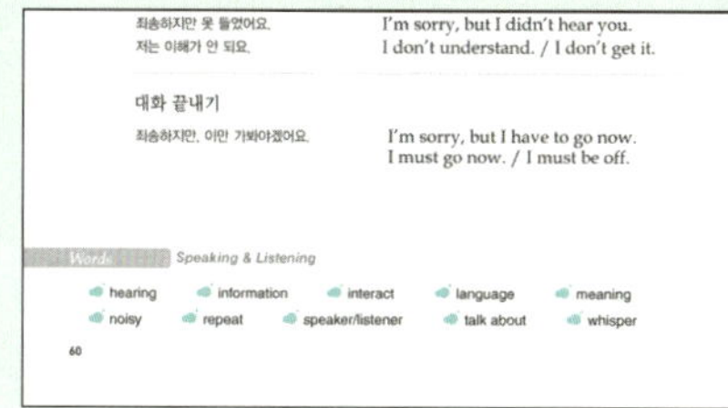

Words

듣기평가에서 자주 출제되는 특정 주제의 중요 어휘를 익힙니다.

03

Check Up

01–02. 앞서 배운 의사소통 기능을 중심으로 구성된 짧은 내용을 듣고, 간단한 연습 문제를 풀어봅니다.

03. 빈칸에 알맞은 의사소통 표현을 써 보면서 해당 표현들을 확실히 기억합니다.

04

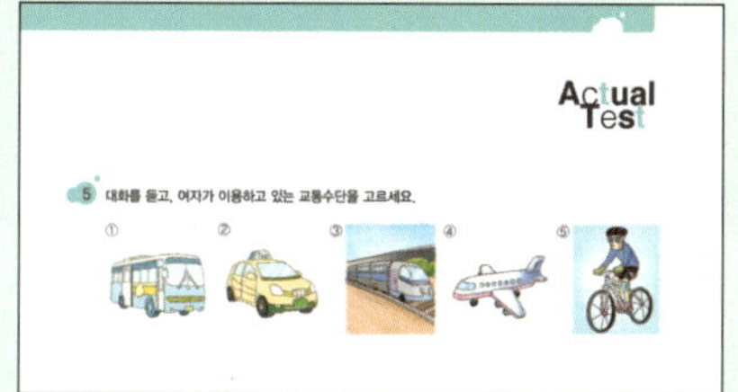

Actual Test

핵심 의사소통 기능을 포함한 내용으로 구성된 8문항의 문제를 풀어봅니다. 다양한 유형의 실전 듣기평가 문제 유형을 익힐 수 있습니다.

05

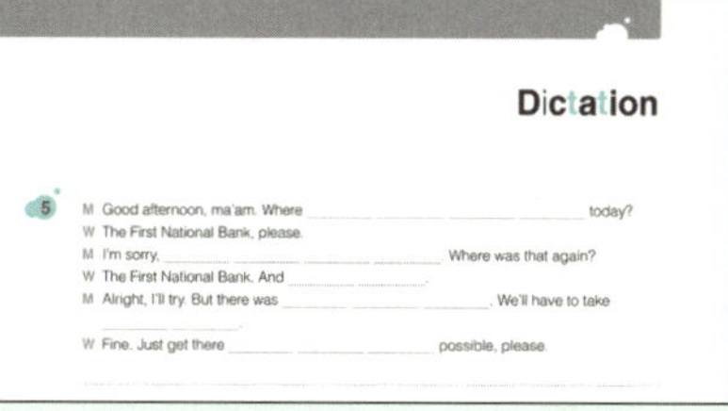

Dictation

Actual Test 8문항의 스크립트를 다시 듣고 빈칸을 채우면서 주요 표현과 어휘를 복습합니다.

06

모의고사

실전과 형태로 구성된 총 3회의 모의고사를 통해 실제 듣기평가 시험에 완벽 대비합니다.

Table of Contents

A Separate-Volume Supplement : Answers and Audio scripts . MP3 File CD

I MAY I HAVE THIS?

허락 요청하기

~을 해도 되나요?	May I ~? / Can I ~?
~을 하도록 허락해 주시겠어요?	Can you allow me to ~?
~을 하게 해주세요.	Let me ~, please.
~을 하는 방법/시간/장소를 알려주세요.	Let me know how/when/where to ~.

허락요청에 답하기

물론이지요.	Yes, you can/may. / Of course. Sure, go ahead. / Sure, why not? That's fine with me. / Sure, no problem. Feel free to do so.
죄송하지만, 안돼요.	No, you can't/may not. I'm sorry, you can't. / Sorry, but ~. I'm afraid you can't.

Words   *Neighbor*

 come by    friendly    get along with    housewarming    move in

 neighborhood    next-door    throw a party    village   visitor

 대화를 듣고, 뒤에 이어질 남자의 행동으로 알맞은 그림을 골라 ✓ 표 하세요.

 대화를 듣고, 내용과 일치하면 T, 일치하지 않으면 F에 ✓ 표 하세요.

1 The girl wants to have a party next weekend. T F
2 The girl's dad wants her to clean her room. T F

03 주어진 표현을 사용하여 대화를 완성하세요.

fine with me	Feel free to do so
can I go and take	Let me know

A Uncle Tom, _________________ some pictures of your house?
It's for my art class.
B _________________.
A Oh, thank you. _________________ when I can visit you.
Can I visit you at 2 p.m.?
B That's _________________.

들려주는 내용을 잘 듣고 물음에 답하세요.

1 다음 그림의 상황에 맞는 대화를 고르세요.

①   ②   ③   ④   ⑤

2 대화를 듣고, 남자가 학교에 가기 싫어하는 이유를 고르세요.

① 학교에서 따돌림을 당해서   ② 선생님이 무서워서

③ 잠을 더 자고 싶어서   ④ 컴퓨터 게임을 하고 싶어서

⑤ 수업이 재미 없어서

3 대화를 듣고, 대화가 일어나고 있는 장소를 고르세요.

①  ②  ③  ④  ⑤ 

4 다음을 듣고, 여자가 전화를 건 이유를 고르세요.

① 저녁 메뉴를 정하려고   ② 마중을 나오라고 하려고

③ 저녁을 먹었는지 확인하려고   ④ 저녁을 준비하라고 부탁하려고

⑤ 집에 누가 있는지 확인하려고

5 대화를 듣고, 남자의 말에 이어질 여자의 응답으로 알맞은 것을 고르세요.

> W ____

① No, you can't.
② I can't agree with you.
③ Sure, no problem.
④ I'm sorry, but I don't know it well.
⑤ I'm happy to hear that.

6 다음을 듣고, 무엇에 관한 내용인지 고르세요.

① 우주캠프 준비물 공지　　② 우주캠프 참가자 모집　　③ 다양한 여름 캠프 소개
④ 우주캠프 일정 안내　　⑤ 캠프 참가시 유의사항 안내

7 대화를 듣고, 메모의 내용이 <u>잘못된</u> 것을 고르세요.

> Attention all Club Members:
>
> ① Club Meeting: Thursday
> ② Regarding: New Computers
> ③ Meeting will be from 11 to 1
> ④ Will Order Lunch During Meeting
> ⑤ Bring $5 for Lunch

8 대화를 듣고, 여자의 문제가 무엇인지 고르세요.

① 시험 성적이 향상하지 않는다.　② 진로를 결정하지 못했다.　③ 수업 시간에 잠을 잔다.
④ 교우 관계가 좋지 않다.　⑤ 선생님들에게 반항을 한다.

다음을 듣고 빈칸에 들어갈 알맞은 말을 쓰세요.

1

① M ___________ ___________ ___________ the dog, Mom?
 W No, you may not. It might be dangerous.
② M Ms. Cooper, ___________ ___________ ___________ sit closer to the chalkboard?
 I'm having trouble seeing it.
 W Yes, you ___________ ___________ ___________ .
③ M Can I use your computer ___________ ___________ ___________ ? I need to check my
 e-mail.
 W ___________ ___________ to use my computer.
④ W Can I use your cell phone ___________ ___________ ___________ ?
 M ___________ , ___________ ___________ .
⑤ W Please ___________ ___________ ___________ if I can borrow your science book tonight.
 M Sure, go ahead. I ___________ ___________ to study it today.

2

M Mom, ___________ ___________ ___________ ___________ today?
W I'm afraid you can't. Is ___________ ___________ ___________ ?
M It's just... I hate going to school every day. It's so boring. I ___________ ___________ ___________
 ___________ . I don't know what to do.
W David, thank you for telling me that. I'll help you ___________ ___________ ___________ . Let's
 study them together, starting today.

3

W Dad, may I ___________ ___________ ___________ home with me?
M No, you may not. We only ___________ ___________ ___________ for some more
 goldfish.
W But he's so cute! I promise I'll ___________ ___________ ___________ ___________ him.
M You can ___________ ___________ ___________ ___________ about it later.
 But we're only buying ___________ ___________ ___________ today.

4

W Hi, it's me, honey. I will be home ___________ ___________ ___________ ___________ this
 evening. I was wondering ___________ ___________ ___________ to do for dinner. Let me know
 if ___________ ___________ ___________ ___________ something to eat for you. I can get a pizza
 or something else ___________ ___________ ___________ ___________ , if you'd like. Talk to you
 later. Love you!

5

M Ellen, can I ______ ______ ______ ______? I left mine at the school.

W ______ ______ ______ ______ it. I just need it back by tomorrow morning.

M Thanks. I have a big test tomorrow. ______ ______ ______ ______ ______, I'm a little nervous.

W What is your test going ______ ______ ______?

M Some geometry formulas.

W Well, I can help you, ______ ______ ______. I am pretty good ______ ______ ______.

M Then can you see me tonight?

6

M ______ ______ ______ ______ about space camp. It's ______ ______ ______ summer camp in the country! Here, you learn all about space, planets, and rocket ships! You can talk to people ______ ______ ______ ______! They'll tell you what it's like to ______ ______ ______ ______. You can even play special video games ______ ______ ______. So join us today!

7

M Janice, is there going to be a club meeting on Thursday?

W Yeah. It's ______ ______ ______ ______ the new computers. ______ ______ ______ from 11 to 1.

M Great. May I make a short presentation during the meeting? I'll show the new members ______ ______ ______ some programs on the new computers.

W Yes, you ______ ______ ______ ______. In fact, I think that's a good idea.

M Cool. Oh, and I heard we were ordering lunch. ______ ______ ______ should we bring for the lunch order?

W Please bring $7. ______ ______ ______ everything.

8

M Lisa, ______ ______ ______ ______ you a minute?

W Sure, what is it?

M I had a little chat with Mr. Murphy yesterday afternoon.

W ______ ______ ______ ______ you?

M He said that you ______ ______ ______ in his class.

W I'm sorry, Dad. I try to stay awake, but I ______ ______ ______ all the time.

M Well, that is not ______ ______ ______. Every student has to study at school.

W I'm so sorry.

 WHO'S CALLING?

전화 걸기

~와 통화 할 수 있나요?	Can I talk to ~? / May I speak with ~? Is ~ available?
전데요.	Speaking. / This is ~ speaking.
메시지 좀 전해주시겠어요?	Can I leave a message?

전화 받기

전화거신 분은 누구세요?	Who's calling, please?
전화 잘못 거셨어요.	You've dialed the wrong number. You have the wrong number.
잠시만요, 바꿔 드릴게요.	Hold on/Wait a second, I'll get ~.
메시지를 남기시겠어요?	Would you like to leave a message?

Words   **Communication**

- body language
- call back
- cell phone
- contact
- conversation
- give ~ a call
- keep in touch
- speech
- text message

01 대화를 듣고, 남자가 이야기 하고 있는 동물을 골라 ✓ 표 하세요.

a

b

c

02 대화를 듣고, 맞는 것에 ✓ 표 하세요.

The woman hung up the phone because

☐ she had to take another call.
☐ she dialed the wrong number.
☐ she became angry at the man.

03 주어진 표현을 사용하여 대화를 완성하세요.

| who's calling | Is Karen there |
| Hold on, I'll get | This is her classmate |

A Hello. _______________________?
B May I ask _______________________, please?
A _______________________, Timothy.
B _______________________ her for you.
A Thank you.

들려주는 내용을 잘 듣고 물음에 답하세요.

1 대화를 듣고, 은행의 위치를 고르세요.

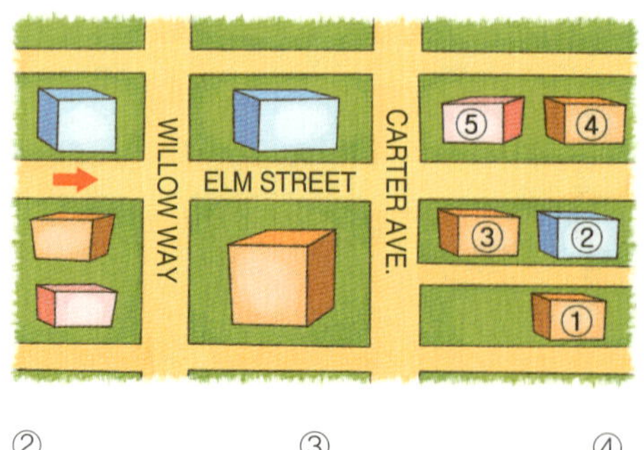

①   ②   ③   ④   ⑤

2 다음을 듣고, 여자에 대해 알 수 <u>없는</u> 내용을 고르세요.

① 유럽 여행 중이다.
② 다음 주 금요일에 돌아올 것이다.
③ 통화는 할 수 없다.
④ 메일 확인은 못 할 것이다.
⑤ 자동 응답 모드를 설정해 두었다.

3 대화를 듣고, 상황을 가장 잘 설명한 것을 고르세요.

① 남자는 친구와 함께 놀기를 원한다.
② 남자는 여자에게 혼이 나고 있다.
③ 남자는 친구에게 필기공책을 빌리려고 한다.
④ 남자는 여자에게 조언을 구하고 있다.
⑤ 남자는 친구와 함께 공부를 하려고 한다.

4 대화를 듣고, 남자의 현재 상태를 고르세요.

①  ②  ③  ④  ⑤ 

5 다음을 듣고, 메모의 내용이 <u>잘못된</u> 것을 고르세요.

> ① To: Mr. Walker
> ② Son's science teacher called
> ③ Son has missed class for three days
> ④ Teacher wants a meeting
> ⑤ Call her back at 834-0987

6 대화를 듣고, 여자에 대해 알 수 <u>없는</u> 것을 고르세요.

① 나이   ② 상품 사용 유무   ③ 주소
④ 상품 구매 빈도수   ⑤ 상품에 대한 만족도

7 대화를 듣고, 여자가 전화를 건 이유를 고르세요.

① 의약품에 대한 정보를 얻으려고
② 고객에게 상품구매를 유도하려고
③ 남자의 부인에게 건강상태를 확인하려고
④ 고객에게 약을 찾아가라고 하려고
⑤ 남자의 딸을 위해 구급차를 불러주려고

8 대화를 듣고, 여자의 말에 이어질 남자의 응답으로 알맞은 것을 고르세요.

M _______________________

① Wait a second. I'll get him.
② There's no Heath here.
③ I'm sorry, but he's not around.
④ Who's calling, please?
⑤ Sorry, you have the wrong number.

1

M Hello, is this the First National Bank?

W Yes, it is. __________ __________ __________ __________ you, sir?

M I want to know __________ __________ __________. My Internet is down, so I can't __________ __________ __________ there.

W No problem, sir. Drive east on Elm Street. __________ __________ __________ Carter Avenue, and then take your first left.

M So the bank will be __________ __________ __________, then?

W Yes, sir. It will be the second building __________ __________ __________.

2

W Hi, __________ __________ Clara. You've reached my answering machine. Sorry, I can't __________ __________ __________ __________ right now. I'm on vacation in Europe. __________ __________ __________ next Friday. Please leave your name and number. I'll contact you __________ __________ __________ __________. You can send me messages through e-mail, though. Thanks, and talk to you later!

3

M Hello. I need to speak with Charlie. __________ __________ __________?

W __________ __________, please?

M This is Bob. I have the same chemistry class as Charlie. __________ __________ yesterday's class and I wanted to __________ __________ __________ from him tomorrow.

W Hold on, please. __________ __________ __________.

4

M Hello, this is Mike Sanders. Is Dr. Stephens available?

W Dr. Stephens? I'm sorry, but he just stepped out. Would you like to __________ __________ __________?

M Yes, please. I bought __________ __________ __________ __________ two days ago. Then __________ __________ __________ broke out and my skin started __________ __________ __________. I don't know what to do.

W Oh, that must be hard for you. I'll tell him __________ __________ __________ __________.

M Thank you.

5

W Hello, Mr. Walker. _________ _______ your son's English teacher, Ms. Harris. _________ ________ because your son has missed _________ _________ _________ _________ recently. He has not attended class _________ _________ _________. I have not been able _________ _________ _________ _________ about this. I think we need to have a meeting _________ _________ _________. Please _________ _________ _________ at my office at 834-0987.

6

M Hello, _________ _________ Johnson Cosmetics. We're calling some customers _________ _________ _________ _________. It will only take a moment.

W OK.

M Great. _________ _________ _________ how old you are?

W 15.

M Uh-huh. And how often do you _________ _________ _________?

W Every few months.

M OK. And have you _________ _________ _________ with these products?

W No. they were all fine.

M Great. That's _________ _________ _________. Thank you for your time.

7

W Hello, is Ms. Carol Summers there?

M _________ _________, please?

W This is Rachel at Stoker's Pharmacy.

M Oh. Well, Carol _________ _________ _________ _________. This is her dad. Can I _________ _________ _________ for her?

W Yes, Mr. Summers. Her medicine is ready _________ _________ _________. I'm calling to let her know.

M Great, _________ _________ _________ when she gets back. Thank you.

8

M Hello?

W Hi, Carlton. It's Jane. _________ _________ _________ tonight? I got _________ _________ _________.

M I'm sorry, but I have an important presentation tomorrow.

W Oh. Well, what about _________ _________, Heath? _________ _________ _________?

M Yes, he _________ _________ _________.

W Great! Can I talk to him?

UNIT II I CAN'T WAIT!

소망/기대 말하기

나는 ~했으면 좋겠어요.	I hope/wish to ~. I hope/wish that ~. It will be nice to ~.
나는 ~을 기대하고 있어요.	I'm looking forward to ~.
나는 ~이 너무나 기다려져요.	I can't wait to ~.
나는 ~을 (정말) 하고 싶어요.	I (really) want to ~. / I'd like to ~.

의지/계획 말하기

나는 ~을 할 거에요.	I've decided to ~. / I'm going to ~. I'm planning to ~.

- celebration
- dress up
- enjoy
- favorite
- guest
- interesting
- prepare
- present
- stay up
- stylish

01 대화를 듣고, 여자의 할머니를 골라 ✓ 표 하세요.

02 대화를 듣고, 내용과 일치하도록 괄호 안에서 알맞은 말을 고르세요.

1 Rick is planning to (buy, rent) a new couch next week.
2 Linda will help Rick buy a (regular, stylish) couch.

03 주어진 표현을 사용하여 대화를 완성하세요.

I'm looking forward to I can't wait to	I hope to go planning to go to

A __________________________ the next *Harry Potter* book.
B Me, too. __________________________ read it.
A I'm also __________________________ see the movie next month.
B It sounds good. __________________, too.

들려주는 내용을 잘 듣고 물음에 답하세요.

1 다음 그림의 상황을 계획하고 있는 대화를 고르세요.

①   ②   ③   ④   ⑤

2 대화를 듣고, 여자가 남자에게 한 조언을 고르세요.

① He should not enter the essay contest.
② He should write a very long essay.
③ He should choose a proper topic.
④ He should spend much time writing.
⑤ He should enter a speech contest.

3 대화를 듣고, 하이킹을 가게 될 인원이 몇 명인지 고르세요.

① 2명   ② 3명   ③ 4명   ④ 5명   ⑤ 6명

4 다음을 듣고, 여자가 고대하는 날이 무엇인지 고르세요.

① 휴일   ② 졸업식   ③ 결혼기념일   ④ 휴가   ⑤ 생일

5 다음을 듣고, 글의 종류가 무엇인지 고르세요.

① 편지　　　　　　② 보고서　　　　　　③ 연설문
④ 안내문　　　　　　⑤ 일기

6 대화를 듣고, 관계 깊은 속담을 고르세요.

① There's no smoke without fire.
② Don't put the cart before the horse.
③ A friend in need is a friend indeed.
④ Hope is the poor man's bread.
⑤ Love will find a way.

7 대화를 듣고, 대화에서 언급되지 <u>않은</u> 것을 고르세요.

① 영화의 후기　　　　② 영화의 출연배우　　　　③ 영화 개봉일
④ 약속 시간　　　　　⑤ 영화의 장르

8 대화를 듣고, 포스터의 내용과 일치하지 <u>않는</u> 것을 고르세요.

① Electric Fire Band
② Friday night, 8:30
③ At the West End Cafe
④ Four new songs will be played
⑤ Tickets are just $6

다음을 듣고 빈칸에 들어갈 알맞은 말을 쓰세요.

1

① W ________ ________ ________ ________ the next train to the downtown marketplace.

   M Well, ________ ________ ________ ________ for another 10 minutes.

② M ________ ________ ________ for next week?

   W Yeah. I'm looking forward to ________ ________ ________.

③ M ________ ________ ________ ________ some surfing at the beach on Sunday. ________ ________ ________?

   W Sorry. I have other plans.

④ M Would you like to ________ ________ ________ this weekend?

   W Sure. ________ ________ ________ ________ some of the beautiful countryside.

⑤ W I'm planning ________ ________ ________ tomorrow. Care to join?

   M Sorry, I can't. I have to ________ ________ ________.

2

W Good morning, Todd. Did you want to speak to me?

M Yes, Ms. Hoover. ________ ________ ________ enter that essay contest next month. I'd like to ________ ________ ________. But I don't know what to write about.

W Well, you should write ________ ________ ________. What is your favorite subject?

M Hmm. Probably art.

W Okay. Then just find ________ ________ ________ ________ that into an essay. That's how you ________ ________ ________.

M Thanks. I'll try doing that.

3

W Well, it looks like ________ ________ ________ for me.

M Really? You don't have any plans?

W No. I want ________ ________ ________ and do something else.

M Well, ________ ________ ________ go hiking this Sunday. ________ ________ to join us if you like.

W Who are ________ ________ ________?

M My roommates, Timmy and Mike.

W Then can ________ ________ ________, too?

M Sure, why not? ________ ________ ________!

4

W I'm ________ ________ ________ this Saturday. A lot of my friends are coming to see me. ________ ________ ________ ________ lots of games, watch movies, and ___________ ___________ _________. I'll be getting a lot of presents, too. It's to celebrate _________ ___________ _________. I always love these occasions. It's just too bad they only happen ___________ ___________ _________.

5

M My name is Harold Gates, and I am a middle school student. It has always been my dream to attend your academy. I have ___________ ___________ _________ in my class, and I am a very hard worker. I ___________ ___________ _________ six clubs at my school. ___________ ___________ _________ an essay and recommendation with this. _________ ___________ ___________ _________ hearing from your school. Thank you.

6

M Hey, Ellen. Do you think Tara ___________ ___________ _________ dancing?

W I don't know. Why ___________ ___________ _________?

M Well, I've decided ___________ ___________ ___________ _________ on a date, but I'm not sure ___________ ___________ ___________ _________. I mean, I'd like to go out dancing somewhere. But she might like ___________ ___________ _________. I don't like going to movies, though.

W See ___________ ___________ _________ "yes," first.

M Right. ___________ ___________ ___________ _________ her out first.

7

M Hey, Alicia, ___________ ___________ _________ about that new comedy with Brad Pitt?

W Yeah. I ___________ ___________ _________ it. But I'm not sure when ___________ _________ _________. Do you know when that is?

M I think it's opening this Saturday. Would you ___________ ___________ _________ _________ it with me?

W Well, sure. I'd really like that, Dale.

M Great. I'll ___________ ___________ _________ at 6 o'clock, then.

8

M ___________ ___________ _________ for that Electric Fire Band show Friday night. Are you going?

W ___________ _________. How much are tickets?

M They're just $5. And the band is ___________ ___________ _________ four new songs!

W Wow. That might be ___________ ___________ _________. Where's the show?

M It's at the West End Cafe. The show starts at 8:30.

W Yeah, that sounds ___________ _________. I'm looking forward to it.

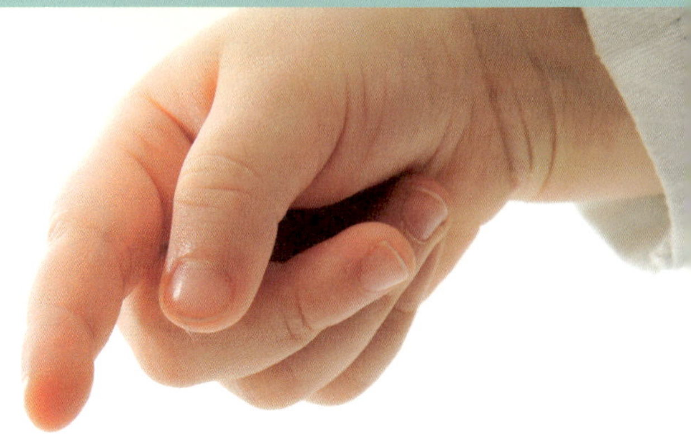

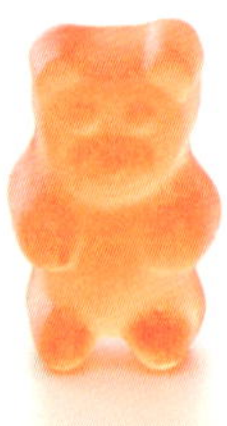

IV WHAT'S YOUR FAVORITE COLOR?

원하는 것 묻고 답하기

당신은 (그 외에) 무엇을 하고 싶습니까?   What (else) would you like to ~?
　　　　　　　　　　　　　　　　　　 What do you want to ~?

당신은 어떤 종류의 음식을 원하십니까?   What kind of food do you want?

저는 ~을 하길 원해요.   I would[I'd] like to ~. / I want to ~.

관심 묻고 답하기

당신이 가장 좋아하는 ~은 무엇입니까?   What's your favorite ~?

당신은 ~에 관심이 있습니까?   Are you interested in ~?

저는 ~을 좋아합니다/관심이 있습니다.   My favorite is ~. / I enjoy ~. / I like ~.
　　　　　　　　　　　　　　　　 I'm interested in ~.

제가 가장 좋아하는 음식은 ~입니다.   My favorite food is ~.

Words	*Behavior*

 fill out　 finish　 focus on　 give up　 go through

 hire　 offer　 prepare　 return　 sign up　 stop by

24

01 대화를 듣고, 여자가 이동할 경로의 순서를 적으세요.

______ ➡ ______ ➡ ______

02 대화를 듣고, 두 사람이 각각 좋아하는 영화장르를 고르세요.

1 Woman ·   　·ⓐ Horror

　　　　　　　·ⓑ Romantic Comedy

2 Man　·   　·ⓒ Action

03 주어진 표현을 사용하여 대화를 완성하세요.

My favorite type is	I enjoy reading
I'm interested in	What is your favorite

A __________________ type of book?

B Hmm. __________________ fiction. __________________ fictional characters. What about you?

A __________________ mystery novels.

들려주는 내용을 잘 듣고 물음에 답하세요.

1 대화를 듣고, 남자가 무엇을 사려고 하는지 고르세요.

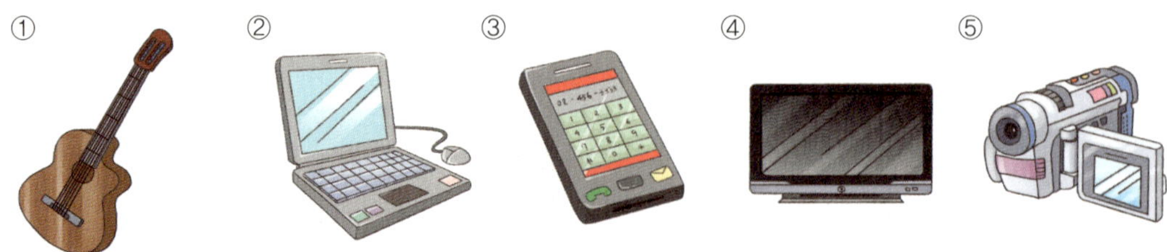

2 대화를 듣고, 남자의 문제가 무엇인지 고르세요.

① He can't prepare a certain recipe.
② He needs to get an operation.
③ He can't enjoy his favorite dish.
④ He needs to lose weight.
⑤ He has a stomachache now.

3 다음을 듣고, 여자가 원하는 생일선물을 고르세요.

① 라디오　　　② 조리도구　　　③ 접시　　　④ 인형　　　⑤ 가방

4 대화를 듣고, 내용이 일치하지 <u>않는</u> 것을 고르세요.

① 수업은 1시간 15분 동안 진행된다.
② 요가 수업은 일 주일에 두 번 있다.
③ 여자는 요가 초보자이다.
④ 여자는 요가를 배워본 경험이 있다.
⑤ 여자는 수업등록을 할 것이다.

5 대화를 듣고, 남자가 어디를 가려고 하는지 고르세요.

① a basketball game   ② a hockey game   ③ a concert
④ a meeting   ⑤ a baseball game

6 대화를 듣고, 남자의 심정으로 알맞은 것을 고르세요.

① concerned   ② curious   ③ disappointed
④ excited   ⑤ scared

7 대화를 듣고, 관계 깊은 속담을 고르세요.

① Like father, like son.
② Time flies when you're having fun.
③ Good health is above wealth.
④ No bees, no honey.
⑤ It takes two to tango.

8 다음을 듣고, 스케줄 표와 일치하지 <u>않는</u> 요일을 고르세요.

Class Schedule

Monday	Tuesday	Wednesday	Thursday	Friday
Pick Topics for Projects	Review for Biology Test	Biology Test	Watch Video	HOLIDAY

① Monday   ② Tuesday   ③ Wednesday   ④ Thursday   ⑤ Friday

다음을 듣고 빈칸에 들어갈 알맞은 말을 쓰세요.

1

W I heard that you sold a lot of your personal belongings.
M Yeah. I __________ __________ __________ __________ my old books and movies. I made about $200.
W Cool. What do you want __________ __________ __________ __________?
M Well, my cell phone is __________ __________ __________. I'd like to buy one of those __________ __________ __________.
W Yeah. You could get __________ __________ __________ __________ with all that money.
M I __________ __________ __________.

2

W What's __________ __________ __________, Jack?
M Hmm. I love gumbo.
W What's gumbo?
M It's __________ __________ __________ made with shrimp, sausage, rice, and a lot of __________ __________. But I can't eat it much anymore.
W Why not?
M Well, I __________ __________ __________ on my stomach recently. My doctor says I have to __________ __________ __________ __________ for a while.
W Oh, I'm sorry.

3

W My favorite TV show is Cooking Contest. I want __________ __________ __________ __________, and this show teaches __________ __________ __________ some amazing dishes. I always want to __________ __________ __________, but I don't have all the necessary __________ __________. My birthday is __________ __________ __________, though. My parents said they will buy me __________ __________ __________ for my birthday. So I'd like to ask __________ __________ __________ for my birthday.

4

W Excuse me, I'd like __________ __________ __________ for a class.
M No problem. __________ __________ __________ __________ would you like to join?
W Yoga, please.
M Is this your first time __________ __________?
W I'd have to say so. I've only attended __________ __________ __________.
M Then you're in beginner's level.
W __________ __________ __________ for that?

M Classes are on Monday from 5:15 p.m. to 6: 30 p.m.

W That's fine. ___________ ___________ ___________ for it.

5

W Hey, Jack. What's your favorite sport?

M ___________ ___________ ___________ is hockey.

W Oh, I didn't know you ___________ ___________ .

M Yeah. In fact, I wanted to be a hockey player when I was a kid. ___________ ___________ ___________ in hockey, too?

W No, I ___________ ___________ . There is actually a game tonight. You can ___________ ___________ ___________ if you want.

M Sure, I'd love to.

6

M Well, Cindy. I'm going to ___________ ___________ ___________ next year.

W Really? Well, we're going ___________ ___________ ___________ here.

M Oh, I'm ___________ ___________ ___________ . I would like to see you guys ___________ ___________ ___________ ___________ . But I also look forward to making new friends, too.

W Yeah. ___________ ___________ that will be nice.

M Yeah. It's going ___________ ___________ ___________ !

7

W Well, Timmy, it's almost time to leave. What else ___________ ___________ ___________ to see at the amusement park?

M Well, I'd like ___________ ___________ ___________ that roller coaster again.

W That's fine.

M Can we also ___________ ___________ the gift shop? And can we ___________ ___________ the haunted house?

W Timmy, we have to leave soon. We've already been here for 6 hours!

M Aww. ___________ ___________ ___________ . I was having such a good time.

8

W Okay, everyone. Let's ___________ ___________ ___________ ___________ our schedule for next week. Monday we're selecting topics for our projects. ___________ ___________ ___________ to think carefully about those. Those are due next month. Also, you know you have a biology test on Wednesday. We'll have ___________ ___________ ___________ for that on Tuesday. Thursday we will go ___________ ___________ ___________ ___________ research for our project. And of course, there is ___________ ___________ on Friday.

UNIT V OH, I APOLOGIZE!

사과하기

(∼해서) 죄송해요.	I'm sorry (to ∼/that ∼). / I apologize (for ∼).
(∼을) 용서해 주세요.	Please forgive me (for ∼).
제 실수였어요.	It was my fault.

사과에 답하기

괜찮아요.	That's OK. / That's all right. / Never mind. No problem. / Forget it. / It doesn't matter.

불만 표현하기

그건 불공평해요.	That's/It's not fair.

Words   *Time*

- be about to
- charge
- due
- enough
- fine
- in a minute
- in time
- overdue
- right away
- timely

01 대화를 듣고, 남자가 가게 될 장소를 골라 ✓ 표 하세요.

02 대화를 듣고, 내용과 일치하면 T, 일치하지 않으면 F에 ✓ 표 하세요.

1 The man was not going to buy a DVD recorder. T F
2 The store doesn't sell DVD recorders. T F

03 주어진 표현을 사용하여 대화를 완성하세요.

| Never mind | That's OK |
| Oh, I'm sorry | apologize for that |

A Did you pick up the groceries I asked you to get?
B _________________, I forgot. I _________________.
A _________________.
B Well, should I go buy something now?
A _________________. I'll try to cook something up.

들려주는 내용을 잘 듣고 물음에 답하세요.

1 대화를 듣고, 대화가 일어나고 있는 장소를 고르세요.

① 서점　　　　② 백화점　　　　③ 식당　　　　④ 영화관　　　　⑤ 도서관

2 대화를 듣고, 두 사람의 관계로 알맞은 것을 고르세요.

① 의사 – 환자　　　　② 상사 – 직원　　　　③ 교사 – 학생
④ 엄마 – 아들　　　　⑤ 점원 – 고객

3 대화를 듣고, 남자가 여자에게 말을 건 이유를 고르세요.

① To order his food
② To complain about his food
③ To pay his bill
④ To take her order
⑤ To ask for water

4 대화를 듣고, 여자가 이용하고 있는 교통수단을 고르세요.

①　②　③　④　⑤

5 대화를 듣고, 대화와 일치하는 내용을 고르세요.

① 여자는 남자에게 돈을 주었다.
② 남자에게는 낡은 재킷이 있었다.
③ 남자는 여자에게 재킷을 사 주었다.
④ 남자는 여자의 재킷을 잃어버렸다.
⑤ 여자의 삼촌은 그녀에게 재킷을 줄 것이다.

6 다음을 듣고, 그림 상황에 맞는 대화를 고르세요.

①   ②   ③   ④   ⑤

7 대화를 듣고, 여자의 심정으로 알맞은 것을 고르세요.

① ashamed   ② tired   ③ angry
④ worried   ⑤ excited

8 다음을 듣고, 여자가 불만을 표현하는 이유를 고르세요.

① 경기에서 아쉽게 승리를 하지 못해서
② 팀의 다른 선수들과 의견충돌이 생겨서
③ 여자보다 더 어린 선수가 팀의 주장이 되어서
④ 부상으로 인해 경기에 참가하지 못하게 되어서
⑤ 아무리 노력해도 실력이 늘지를 않아서

다음을 듣고 빈칸에 들어갈 알맞은 말을 쓰세요.

1

M Hey. I'm here to return this book.

W Okay, sir. Oh, this book is __________ __________ __________. There's a __________ __________ __________ on it.

M What? __________ __________ __________! I couldn't return it earlier because I was __________ __________ __________!

W There's no fine __________ __________ __________ __________. After that, though, you need to pay ten cents a day. I'm sorry.

M Never mind. I'll just __________ __________ __________.

2

W Terry, __________ __________ __________ your chemistry paper yesterday.

M __________ __________, Ms. Hines. __________ __________ __________ __________ finish it in time because of my operation last week.

W That's OK. But you should have __________ __________ __________ sooner. I'll give you until Friday __________ __________ __________.

M Thanks. That should be __________ __________.

3

M Excuse me, miss? This steak __________ __________ __________ for me.

W I don't understand. __________ __________ __________ it cooked well done?

M Actually, no. I __________ __________ for medium rare. I like my steak to be __________ __________ __________.

W Oh, that's right. __________ __________, sir. I'll go back and __________ __________ __________ __________ you a new steak, right away.

4

M __________ __________ __________, ma'am?

W Actually, my suitcase is up there, but I am not able __________ __________ __________.

M Oh, I'm sorry. Here, __________ __________ __________ __________ with that.

W Thanks. Also, when will __________ __________ __________ on this flight?

M Not for a few hours. But we can get you __________ __________ __________ and some water in a minute, if you want.

W Thank you. __________ __________ __________.

5

W Um, Gerald? __________ __________ __________. I accidentally lost that jacket __________ __________ __________. I'm sorry.

M __________ __________. It was old and __________ __________ anyway.

W Yeah, but I still __________ __________ about it. Listen, I can pay for a new one, if you like.

M Thanks, but that __________ __________ __________ __________. I think my uncle will give me __________ __________ __________.

6

① **M** I'm sorry __________ __________ your cell phone. It was __________ __________.

　W What? How could you do that?

② **M** Hey, __________ __________ __________ that Mike won the prize this time?

　W That's not fair! I also __________ __________ __________!

③ **M** __________ __________ that I didn't call you last night.

　W __________ __________ __________. I went to sleep early.

④ **M** I'm sorry, Jessica. __________ __________ your MP3 player.

　W __________ __________. I was going to buy a new one.

⑤ **M** Mom, __________ __________ __________ for my test results.

　W That's OK. You just need __________ __________ __________.

7

M Hey, Janet. Did you want to talk to me?

W Yes! __________ __________ __________ that yesterday was my birthday? Why didn't you come to my party, Mark? I was really hoping you'd show up.

M I'm sorry. I forgot __________ __________ __________.

W What? How could you do that? I thought you were one of __________ __________ __________!

M Yeah, I know. I don't know how it happened.

W This is unbelievable! I'm __________ __________ in you!

8

W Last week I __________ __________ for my school's volleyball team. I did really well. In fact, I was __________ __________ anyone else there. I was going to be __________ __________ __________, but something happened. I __________ __________ __________ __________ yesterday and badly broke my arm. Now I can't play this year at all. __________ __________ __________! I was looking forward to this for a long time.

VI MAY I TAKE YOUR ORDER?

음식 주문 받기

주문하시겠어요?

May / Can I take your order?
Are you ready to order?

드시고 가시겠습니까,
아니면 포장해드릴까요?

For here or to go?

스테이크 굽기는 어떻게 해드릴까요?

How would you like your steak?

음식 주문하기

~로 주세요.

I'd like to have ~. / I'll have ~.

~로 주시겠어요?

Can I have ~?

여기서 먹고 갈게요 / 포장해주세요.

For here / To go, please.

바짝 / 중간으로 / 살짝 익혀 주세요.

Well done / Medium / Rare, please.

Words　　**Cooking**

- a slice of
- allergic
- appetizer
- discount
- grilled
- meal
-  order
-  restaurant
- take-out
- vegetarian

01 대화를 듣고, 여자가 주문하지 <u>않은</u> 음식에 ✓ 표 하세요.

 a

 b

 c

02 대화를 듣고, 질문에 대한 알맞은 대답에 ✓ 표 하세요.

1 What will the man eat? ☐ grilled steak ☐ pork rib
2 Where is this conversation taking place? ☐ market ☐ restaurant

03 주어진 표현을 사용하여 대화를 완성하세요.

For here or to go	For here, please
Can I take your order	I'd like to have

A Good morning, sir. _____________________?
B Yes, _____________________ pancakes with some coffee, please.
A Of course, sir. _____________________?
B _____________________.

들려주는 내용을 잘 듣고 물음에 답하세요.

1 대화를 듣고, 식당의 위치를 고르세요.

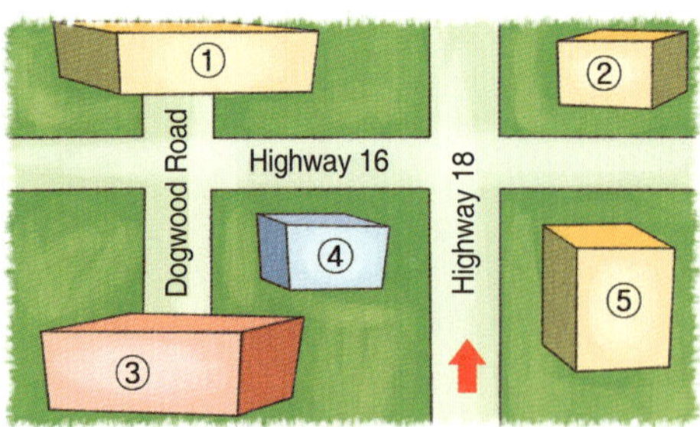

2 대화를 듣고, 이어질 남자의 행동을 고르세요.

① 여자에게 또 다른 메뉴판을 가져다 준다.　② 여자의 주문을 받는다.

③ 여자에게 빵을 가져다 준다.　④ 여자에게 후식을 가져다 준다.

⑤ 여자에게 계산서를 가져다 준다.

3 대화를 듣고, 여자가 주문한 음식의 개수를 고르세요.

① 1개　② 2개　③ 3개　④ 4개　⑤ 5개

4 다음을 듣고, 남자가 주문한 음식을 고르세요.

① 　② 　③  　④ 　⑤ 

5 다음 중 <u>어색한</u> 대화를 고르세요.

①   ②   ③   ④   ⑤

6 대화를 듣고, 남자가 버거를 먹지 <u>않는</u> 이유를 고르세요.

① 매운 음식을 먹지 못해서   ② 버거를 좋아하지 않아서

③ 스테이크를 먹고 싶어서   ④ 새로운 음식을 시도해보고 싶어서

⑤ 단 음식이 먹고 싶어서

7 대화를 듣고, 여자가 먹을 음식의 가격을 고르세요.

MENU			
Pies		**Coffee**	
Cherry	$3.00	Small	$1.50
Peach	$2.00	Medium	$2.00
Blueberry	$2.00	Large	$3.00
Chocolate	$4.00		
Whipped cream	$0.25		

① $3.50   ② $4.00   ③ $4.25   ④ $5.50   ⑤ $6.00

8 대화를 듣고, 남자가 다른 음식을 고르는 이유를 고르세요.

① 남자에게 땅콩 알레르기가 있어서   ② 음식 가격이 너무 비싸서

③ 당일 요리 재료가 다 떨어져서   ④ 다른 음식을 맛보고 싶어서

⑤ 일행이 한 명 더 오기로 해서

1

W　Golden Dragon Chinese Restaurant. This is Christine speaking. May I _________ _________ _________?

M　Yes. _________ _________ _________ _________ two orders of orange chicken, mixed vegetables, and fried rice.

W　All right, sir. It _________ _________ _________ in 20 minutes.

M　Great. I'd like to _________ _________ _________, but I need directions to your restaurant, please.

W　Certainly, sir. Go north on Highway 18. Then turn left on Highway 16. _________ _________ _________ on Dogwood Road. _________ _________ _________ that shopping center.

M　Thank you.

2

M　_________ _________ _________ your order, ma'am?

W　Uh, not yet. I'm _________ _________ for my friend to arrive. But could I possibly _________ _________ _________ for an appetizer?

M　Of course, ma'am. Do you need _________ _________, too?

W　No, that _________ _________ _________. She can just use mine. Thanks anyway.

3

M　May I take your order?

W　Yes. I'd like to have _________ _________ _________ with rice, please.

M　Excellent choice. Now, _________ _________ _________ _________ with this.

W　Let's see. I'll _________ _________ _________ for one of the sides.
　　And _________ _________ _________ _________ do you have today?

M　We have _________ _________ _________ and tomato soup.

W　Okay. I'll have _________ _________ _________, then.

4

W　Hello. My name is Jenny Williams, and I'd like _________ _________ _________ _________. This is for _________. I also have a coupon _________ _________ _________ _________. I'd like two large pizzas, please. I want to have vegetables only _________ _________ _________ _________. The other should be shrimp gold, please.

5

① **M** Can I take your order, ma'am?

W I'll __________ __________ __________, please.

② **W** Can I have a burrito and taco combo, please?

M Yes, ma'am. __________ __________ or to go?

③ **W** __________ __________ __________ to order?

M No, I'd like a few __________ __________ to decide.

④ **W** I'd like to have some shrimp pasta, please.

M Can I take your order?

⑤ **M** __________ __________ __________ __________ your steak, ma'am?

W __________ __________, please.

6

W Hi, __________ __________ Frankie's. are you ready to order?

M Can you __________ __________?

W How about the "volcano burger"? It's __________ __________ but most people love it.

M Well, I think my stomach can't handle __________ __________.

W What about beef steak then? __________ __________ with a baked potato.

M It sounds good. __________ __________ __________.

7

M May I __________ __________ __________, ma'am?

W Yes. I'd like to have __________ __________ __________ __________ and coffee, please.

M __________ __________ __________ __________ would you like?

W Hmm. I think I'll have __________ __________ __________.

M All right. And what size coffee?

W __________ __________ __________. And can I have some whipped cream on the pie, too?

M You got it.

8

M Excuse me. Do you serve any __________ __________ here?

W Yes, sir. We have a special vegetarian section __________ __________ __________.

M Great. How is the Thai vegetable stir fry?

W __________ __________, sir.

M Does it have any peanuts in it? I'm __________ __________ peanuts.

W Oh, yes. The dish has peanuts in it.

M Ah, __________ __________ __________ what other vegetarian dishes you have then.

VII UNIT DO I HAVE TO STUDY?

의무 묻기

| 제가 ~을 해야 하나요? | Should I ~? / Do I have to ~?
 Am I supposed to ~? |

의무 표현하기

저는 ~을 해야 해요.	I (just) have to ~. / I will have to ~.
당신은 ~을 해야 해요.	You're supposed to ~. You have to/must/should ~.
저는 당신이 ~을 해야 한다고 생각해요.	I think you should ~.

금지 표현하기

| 당신은 ~을 하면 안돼요. | You should not/must not/cannot ~.
 You're not supposed to ~. |

Words — Duty

-  be ready for
- complete
- do one's best
- focus on
- from now on
-  keep -ing
-  project
-  submit
-  take time
-  task
- wait in line

01 대화를 듣고, 여자가 각 요일에 할 일을 연결하세요.

1 Monday   **2** Thursday   **3** Friday

02 대화를 듣고, 맞는 것에 ✓ 표 하세요.

The girl missed the school bus today because

☐ she was meeting with her teacher.
☐ she studied until late after school.

03 주어진 표현을 사용하여 대화를 완성하세요.

I think I should	when should I
You have to submit	You have to start

A Hey, _____________________ submit the report?
B _____________________ it by this Friday.
A Then _____________________ start on Thursday.
B What? _____________________ today. You cannot finish it in one day.

들려주는 내용을 잘 듣고 물음에 답하세요.

1 대화를 듣고, 두 사람이 본 표지판을 고르세요.

2 대화를 듣고, 남자의 의견으로 알맞은 것을 고르세요.

① Linda's sister should not quit her job.
② Linda's sister should take the new job.
③ Linda's sister should save her money.
④ Linda's sister should take a job she likes.
⑤ Linda's sister should not get married yet.

3 대화를 듣고, 대화가 일어나고 있는 장소를 고르세요.

① 집　　　　② 교실　　　　③ 호텔　　　　④ 병원　　　　⑤ 식당

4 다음을 듣고, 설명하는 동물이 무엇인지 고르세요.

① bears　　　　② horses　　　　③ cats
④ bats　　　　⑤ elephants

5 다음을 듣고, 어떠한 상황에서 하는 말인지 고르세요.

① 토론　　　　② 상담　　　　③ 뉴스　　　　④ 강의　　　　⑤ 면접

6 다음 그림의 상황에 맞는 대화를 고르세요.

①　　　　②　　　　③　　　　④　　　　⑤

7 대화를 듣고, 여자가 남자를 꾸짖은 이유를 고르세요.

① 남자가 동생과 놀아주지 않아서　　　　② 남자가 그의 방을 어질러놔서
③ 남자가 통금시간을 어겨서　　　　④ 남자가 동생과 싸워서
⑤ 남자가 어린 동생을 괴롭혀서

8 대화를 듣고, 남자가 프로젝트를 끝내야 하는 날짜를 고르세요.

March

Sun	Mon	Tue	Wed	Thu	Fri	Sat
		1	2	3	4	5
6	7	8	9	10	11	12
13	14	15	16	17	18	19

① 4일　　　　② 8일　　　　③ 9일　　　　④ 11일　　　　⑤ 18일

1

M Okay, we've only ___________ ___________ ___________ to get to your school. I'll have to ___________ ___________ ___________.

W Whoa! What are you doing? Didn't you see ___________ ___________ ___________ there? You are ___________ ___________ ___________ there.

M Oh, you're right! ___________ ___________ ___________ at that sign.

W We're lucky, Dad. We didn't hit another car or ___________ ___________ by the police.

2

M Linda, I heard that your sister ___________ ___________ a new job.

W Yeah, but ___________ ___________ ___________ about it. I don't think she will take ___________ ___________ ___________.

M I don't understand. Doesn't it pay a lot more money?

W Yes, but she said she is not ___________ ___________ ___________.

M But she has children. This new job could help support her family. I think ___________ ___________ ___________ it.

W Yeah, you've got ___________ ___________ ___________.

3

M Hi. I ___________ ___________ ___________ for the night.

W Yes, sir. That will be $80, please.

M Okay. Will you take ___________ ___________ ___________?

W Of course, sir. You can watch TV in the lobby, but the Internet ___________ ___________ ___________ now.

M That's fine. When should I ___________ ___________?

W You have to ___________ ___________ by 12:00 p.m., sir.

4

M These very large animals ___________ ___________ ___________ in the woods, mountains, and other places ___________ ___________. They live all over the world. ___________ ___________ ___________ in thick fur, and they can walk ___________ ___________ ___________ or four legs. Some of them sleep during ___________ ___________ ___________. They eat all kinds of things, like fish, berries, honey, and even garbage. You should ___________ ___________ ___________ them because they sometimes attack people.

Dictation

5

W Good morning, everyone. ___________ ___________ ___________, I'd like to ask a question.
Whenever we send a fax, ___________ ___________ ___________ ___________ have an
actual fax machine? ___________ ___________. Today, we're going to learn about new
Internet faxing programs. You can ___________ ___________ very simply with this program.
They also let you ___________ ___________ ___________ faxes through your e-mail address.
If you don't have enough money to buy a fax machine, if you don't know ___________
___________ ___________ one, this will be very useful.

6

① M Mom, ___________ ___________ ___________ ___________ for the exam?
　 W You have to ___________ ___________ ___________ and study for it.
② M You're not ___________ ___________ ___________ your cell phone in the library.
　 W Oh, sorry. I'll take this call outside, then.
③ W You ___________ ___________ ___________ TV before doing your homework.
　 M Okay. I'll start on my homework right away.
④ W Mr. White, am I supposed to ___________ ___________ ___________ by Monday?
　 M Yes, I will not accept late reports.
⑤ W I need to speak with someone right away.
　 M Sorry, ma'am. You must ___________ ___________ ___________ like everyone else here.

7

W Mike, ___________ ___________ ___________ ___________, please.
M What is it, Mom?
W ___________ ___________ ___________ your little brother?
M Well, yeah. But he ___________ ___________ ___________ my toys! I told him to stop, but
___________ ___________.
W That doesn't matter. You're a lot bigger than he is. You ___________ ___________ ___________
him, ever.
M OK, Mom. I'm sorry.

8

W Rudy, did you want to ___________ ___________ me?
M Yes, Ms. Scott. Well, I think I can't ___________ ___________ ___________ by March 8th. It is a
very big project. It will ___________ ___________ ___________ ___________ to finish it.
W I know. I will give you more time. ___________ ___________ ___________. Today is March 4th.
Well, I will allow you to submit the project ___________ ___________ ___________. But
remember this. You have to finish it by then.
M Sure. Thank you.

VIII

U N I T

I DON'T THINK SO.

의견 묻고 답하기

당신은 ~을 어떻게 생각하세요?	What do you think (of / about ~)?
당신은 ~라고 생각하십니까?	Do you think (that) ~?
저는 ~라고 생각해요.	I think (that) ~.

동의하기

저도 같은 생각이에요.	I agree with you. / I think so. / I'm with you.

반대하기

저는 그렇게 생각하지 않아요.	I can't agree with you. / I don't think so. I'm against it.

Words   **Opinion**

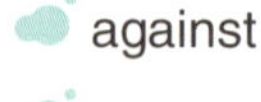 against   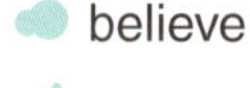 believe   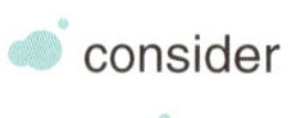 consider   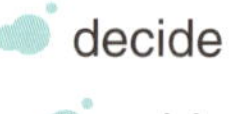 decide   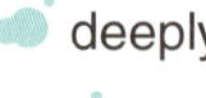 deeply    differ

 greatly    make sense   pretty   subject   the idea of

01 대화를 듣고, 두 사람이 금요일에 할 일을 골라 ✓ 표 하세요.

02 대화를 듣고, 누구의 의견인지 골라 ✓ 표 하세요.

1 Building a restaurant can be a good idea. ☐ man ☐ woman
2 There needs to be a place to play. ☐ man ☐ woman

03 주어진 표현을 사용하여 대화를 완성하세요.

I think it was	Did you find
I'm with you	What did you think

A ________________ today's lecture interesting?
B ________________ pretty interesting. ________________ about it?
A ________________. I usually daydream during class. But I really enjoyed the lecture, too.

들려주는 내용을 잘 듣고 물음에 답하세요.

1 대화를 듣고, 두 사람이 구매하려는 의자를 고르세요.

2 대화를 듣고, 두 사람이 여행에서 즐기지 <u>못한</u> 일을 고르세요.

① 수영　　　　　　② 낚시　　　　　　③ 일광욕
④ 서핑　　　　　　⑤ 조깅

3 다음을 듣고, 마지막에 이어질 말로 알맞은 것을 고르세요.

That is to say, ___________________________________

① I'm with you.　　　　　　② What do you think about it?
③ I agree with you.　　　　　④ Let's discuss this.
⑤ I'm against it.

4 대화를 듣고, 포스터의 내용과 일치하지 <u>않는</u> 것을 고르세요.

Baseball Game

① Braves vs. Cubs　　　　② Wednesday
③ At 6:00 p.m.　　　　　④ All Hot Dogs Half Price
⑤ Come see the stadium's new big TV screen!

5 대화를 듣고, 두 사람이 참석하려는 곳을 고르세요.

① 가족모임　　　　　② 졸업식　　　　　③ 장례식
④ 결혼식　　　　　⑤ 바자회

6 다음을 듣고, 은행에 대해 언급되지 <u>않은</u> 것을 고르세요.

① 수수료를 부과하지 않는다.
② 대출을 받기가 쉽다.
③ 대출 이자가 낮다.
④ 홈페이지가 이용하기에 쉽다.
⑤ 고객만족 서비스를 제공한다.

7 대화를 듣고, 남자의 의견에 대한 여자의 반응을 고르세요.

① 무관심　　　② 동의　　　③ 칭찬　　　④ 반대　　　⑤ 감사

8 대화를 듣고, 대화가 이루어지고 있는 장소를 고르세요.

① 산부인과　　　　　② 이비인후과　　　　　③ 치과
④ 정형외과　　　　　⑤ 안과

1

W What do you think of _________ _________, George?

M Hmm. I think it's _________ _________ _________. I don't want a black couch.

W Well, _________ _________ _________ _________. We need something lighter.

M How about this over here?

W George, that's _________ _________ _________. Two people can't sit on that.

M Ah! This is _________ _________ _________, and it's just the right color, too.

W You're right! I love it.

M I'll see _________ _________ _________ can help us with it.

2

M Well, I had a fun time at the beach this weekend. _________ _________ _________ _________?

W Yeah, _________ _________ _________ _________ for swimming and surfing.

M What did you think _________ _________ _________ there?

W Hmm. Fishing is _________ _________ _________, but I didn't enjoy it much this time.

M _________, _________. There were not many good fishing spots.

3

W Our town has had _________ _________ _________ for nearly 40 years. Now our new mayor wants _________ _________ _________. He says that it costs _________ _________ _________. But this recycling program _________ _________ the amount of trash in our city. We need it _________ _________ _________ and keep the environment clean. That's why I don' t like _________ _________ _________ _________ the program.

4

M That was quite a baseball game! Did you _________ _________ _________, Tammy?

W Oh, I did. The Braves and Cubs played an amazing game. I just wish _________ _________ _________ _________ so late.

M Yeah. 8:00 p.m. is a pretty _________ _________ _________ for a Wednesday night.

W Still, they sold hot dogs _________ _________ _________ tonight. That was pretty nice.

M Yeah. I also liked the new _________ _________ _________ they had. That was _________ _________!

5

M I don't know ______ ______ ______. Do you think it will taste good?

W ______ ______ ______. Everyone loves your cakes.

M Yeah, maybe you're right. There will be ______ ______ ______ ______, anyway.

W Yeah. By the way, I think it's really good ______ ______ ______ ______ once a year.

M ______ ______ ______ ______. It's good to spend time with all of the family members.

6

M Some banks ______ ______ to the customers. Do you think ______ ______?
I don't think so. Here at Eagle Bank, we don't charge you ______ ______. It is also easy ______ ______ ______ ______ with our bank. Plus, our website is very easy to use. We always do our best ______ ______ ______ of our customers. So try Eagle Bank today.

7

W Well, Mr. Moyer isn't ______ ______ ______ this year for our class. ______ ______ ______ ______ of that, Harold?

M I think ______ ______ ______. I mean, I like the parties, but we need the money for ______ ______ ______ like donations for the poor, and so on.

W Sorry, but ______ ______ ______. I mean, those parties are ______ ______ ______ for us. I believe that they make us relax ______ ______ ______.

M Well, maybe we'll ______ ______ ______ next year.

8

M Well, that wasn't too bad. ______ ______ ______ my gums will be OK?

W I think they will be OK. Your two teeth ______ ______ ______.

M That's ______ ______ ______. Thanks for ______ ______ ______ for me, doctor.

W Sure. Just take care of ______ ______ and gums.

WHICH IS SHORTER?

비교하기

A와 B중에 어떤 것이 더 나은 것 같아요?	Which (do you think) is better, A or B? Which do you like better, A or B?
A와 B중에 어떤 색상이 더 나은 것 같아요?	Which color (do you think) is better, A or B? Which color do you like better, A or B?
(제 생각에는) A가 나은 것 같아요.	(I think) A is/looks better.

놀라움 표현하기

그거 놀랍네요.	That's/It's surprising. / That's incredible. That's amazing. / What a surprise.
믿을 수가 없군요.	I can't believe it.

 Career

- dream of
- employee
- employer
- overtime
- promotion
- qualified
- quit
- take a break
- vacation
- work for

 **01** 대화를 듣고, 가장 빠른 순으로 순위를 적으세요.

______ ➡ ______ ➡ ______

02 대화를 듣고, 내용과 일치하는 것에 모두 ✓ 표 하세요.

a The woman doesn't like her school. ☐
b West End Middle School is a public school. ☐
c The woman goes to a private school. ☐

03 주어진 표현을 사용하여 대화를 완성하세요.

Which do you think	looks better on you
I think the red one	the red one or

A I can't decide on a dress. _______________________ is better,
_____________________ the black one?
B _______________________ is better.
A Well, how about the shoes?
B The blue ones __________________________.

들려주는 내용을 잘 듣고 물음에 답하세요.

1 대화를 듣고, 남자의 이모를 고르세요.

①  ②  ③  ④  ⑤ 

2 다음을 듣고, 리조트에 대한 내용과 일치하는 것을 고르세요.

① 사우나에는 아이들은 들어갈 수 없다.
② 어른들을 위해 개방되어 있다.
③ 작지만 아름다운 백사장이 있다.
④ 성인과 아이들을 위한 다양한 시설이 있다.
⑤ 바닷가에서는 놀 수가 없다.

3 다음을 듣고, 이어서 들려주는 질문에 알맞은 대답을 고르세요.

① 14   ② 15   ③ 16   ④ 17   ⑤ 18

4 대화를 듣고, 바로 이어질 남자의 행동으로 알맞은 것을 고르세요.

① 디지털 카메라를 환불할 것이다.   ② 사진을 인화할 것이다.
③ 사진을 찍으러 갈 것이다.   ④ 필름 카메라를 구매할 것이다.
⑤ 다른 디지털 카메라를 살펴볼 것이다.

5 대화를 듣고, 일치하지 <u>않는</u> 내용을 고르세요.

① 여자는 Melissa를 한동안 만나지 못했다.
② Melissa는 지난달에 전액 장학금을 받았다.
③ 여자와 Melissa는 서로 알지 못하는 사이이다.
④ 남자는 어제 Melissa를 만났다.
⑤ Melissa는 공부를 열심히 하는 성실한 학생이다.

6 대화를 듣고, 두 사람이 여행을 떠나는 날짜를 고르세요.

April

Sun	Mon	Tue	Wed	Thu	Fri	Sat
1	2	3	4	5	6	7
8	9	10	11	12	13	14
15	16	17	18	19	20	21
22	23	24	25	26	27	28
29	30					

① 3일   ② 5일   ③ 6일   ④ 10일   ⑤ 12일

7 다음 중 <u>어색한</u> 대화를 고르세요.

①   ②   ③   ④   ⑤

8 대화를 듣고, Sally에 대한 내용으로 맞는 것을 고르세요.

① 절도를 하다가 수감되었다.   ② 자동차를 도난 당했다.
③ 경찰서에 전화를 걸어 자수를 하였다.   ④ 절도범을 직접 체포하였다.
⑤ 도둑이 물건 훔치는 현장을 목격하였다.

다음을 듣고 빈칸에 들어갈 알맞은 말을 쓰세요.

1

M Janice, I'm glad __________ __________ __________ to the party. Say, have you met my aunt?

W I don't think so. Is she here?

M Yeah, she's right over there. She's the woman __________ __________ __________ __________.

W Oh, do you mean that woman __________ __________ __________ __________?

M No, my aunt is __________ __________ that woman.

W Oh, I see her. She's wearing sunglasses, __________ __________?

M Right.

2

M Welcome to the Sandy Shore Vacation Resort. We hope you __________ __________ __________ here. There are several activities for the whole family. We have __________ __________ __________, sauna, and gym for men and women. __________ __________, we have many fun sports programs, __________ __________ __________ and miniature golf. And then there's the highlight __________ __________ __________ – the beach! We have miles and miles __________ __________ __________ and blue ocean! It's bigger __________ __________ __________ beach resort in the country. I'm sure that you will have __________ __________ __________ here!

3

W When I was younger, I dreamed of __________ __________ __________. When I __________ __________, I started growing taller. That got __________ __________ __________. However, that was two years ago, and I've stopped growing now. I'm not very tall, so I __________ __________ __________ __________. Then I was reading about this famous model. I'm actually __________ __________ __________ than she is! __________ __________. This renews my hope.

4

M Excuse me, but I want to buy a new camera. Which do you think is better, this film camera __________ __________ __________ __________?

W Well, the digital camera has __________ __________ that allow different kinds of effects, and it's easier __________ __________ __________ to computers.

M Hmm. That is pretty nice. But I think that's __________ __________ __________. Do you have __________ __________ __________ of digital cameras?

W Of course. Come follow me, and I'll __________ __________ __________ __________.

Dictation

5

M Hey, I saw Melissa yesterday.

W Oh really? I _________ _________ with her _________ _________! How is she doing?

M She's doing really well. She actually got _________ _________ ___________ last month.

W Wow, I can't believe it! I didn't know she was such a _________ _________.

M Yeah. But I think she ___________ _________ because she studies very hard.

W You're right.

6

M Mary, when should _________ _________ _________ our spring vacation?

W I'm not sure. But April would be _________ _________ _________. Which do yo think is better, the first week or _________ _________ _________?

M Hmm. A lot of people will _________ _________ _________ during the first week of April.

W So a lot of them _________ _________ _________ the 6th and 7th. _________ _________ _________ _________ the Thursday before that?

M Sounds great.

7

① M I hit _________ _________ _________ in yesterday's baseball game!

   W Really? _________ _________!

② W Which coffee do you think _________ _________, the Sumatra or the Columbian blend?

   M _________ _________ the Sumatra has a richer flavor.

③ M _________ _________ do you think is better, the red one or the striped one?

   W I think that coat looks _________ _________ _________.

④ W You know something? I'm shorter than _________ _________ _________ now.

   M Wow! _________ _________. He grew up quickly.

⑤ M Did you hear that Ronald got all A's in school?

   W I _________ _________ _________. He didn't study hard this year.

8

W _________ _________ _________ about Sally?

M No, I didn't. What happened to her?

W She helped the police _________ _________ _________!

M Really? _________ _________! How did she do it?

W Well, she saw this guy trying to _________ _________ _________ _________. So she told a policeman about it, and _________ _________ _________ that it was a thief. Then they _________ _________ _________ _________.

M That's good to hear.

U N I T DO YOU GET IT?

다시 묻기와 이해 확인하기

다시 한번 말씀해 주시겠어요?

Would you say that again?
Could you repeat that please?
Could you tell me again?

제 말 이해 하셨어요?

Do you get it? / Do you understand?
Do you get what I mean?

죄송하지만 못 들었어요.
저는 이해가 안 되요.

I'm sorry, but I didn't hear you.
I don't understand. / I don't get it.

대화 끝내기

죄송하지만, 이만 가봐야겠어요.

I'm sorry, but I have to go now.
I must go now. / I must be off.

- hearing
- information
- interact
- language
- meaning
- noisy
- repeat
- speaker/listener
- talk about
- whisper

01 대화를 듣고, 내일의 날씨를 골라 ✓ 표 하세요.

02 대화를 듣고, 질문에 대한 알맞은 대답에 ✓ 표 하세요.

Q Why does the man have to get up early?

A It's because he ☐ has basketball practice.

☐ has baseball practice.

☐ has ballet practice.

03 주어진 표현을 사용하여 대화를 완성하세요.

Did you get that	Can you repeat that, please
I didn't hear you	I'm sorry

A Hello? Mom, it's me. Can you tell me how to get to grandmother's house?

B OK, go west on Wilson Street, and turn right at the second block.

_______________?

A ____________, but ________________. ________________________?

B I said, go west on Wilson Street, and turn right at the second block.

A I got it. Thank you.

들려주는 내용을 잘 듣고 물음에 답하세요.

1 대화를 듣고, 쇼핑몰의 위치를 고르세요.

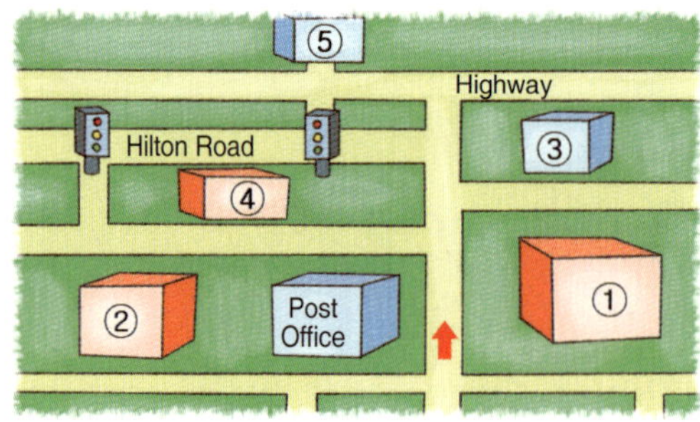

2 다음을 듣고, 여자가 서둘러 전화를 끊은 이유를 고르세요.

① 가스레인지의 불 끄는 것을 깜박해서
② 여자의 엄마가 저녁을 먹으라고 해서
③ 친구와의 약속시간에 늦어서
④ 여자의 엄마가 도움을 요청해서
⑤ 다른 사람이 초인종을 눌러서

3 대화를 듣고, 두 사람의 관계로 알맞은 것을 고르세요.

① waiter – customer
② boyfriend – girlfriend
③ brother – sister
④ teacher – student
⑤ driver – customer

4 대화를 듣고, 남자의 진료예약 시간으로 알맞은 것을 고르세요.

① 1:00 p.m.
② 2:00 p.m.
③ 3:00 p.m.
④ 4:00 p.m.
⑤ 5:00 p.m.

5 대화를 듣고, 여자가 이용하고 있는 교통수단을 고르세요.

①   ②   ③   ④   ⑤

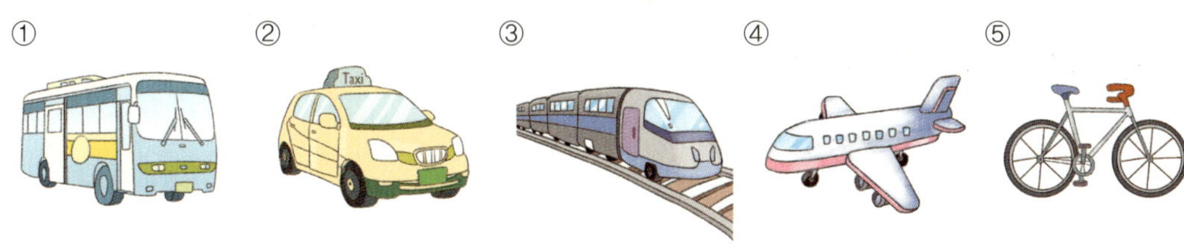

6 대화를 듣고, 여자에게 생긴 일이 무엇인지 고르세요.

① 자신의 룸메이트와 다투었다.　　② 남자친구와 헤어졌다.
③ 휴대폰을 잃어버렸다.　　④ 지갑을 도난 당했다.
⑤ 아파트에 도둑이 들었다.

7 대화를 듣고, 남자가 여자에게 한 조언을 고르세요.

① She should buy new clothes.
② She should not make more friends.
③ She should make more money.
④ She should create a website.
⑤ She should go to a flea market.

8 다음을 듣고, 언급되지 <u>않은</u> 것을 고르세요.

① 소년이 이메일을 쓰는 이유
② 소년이 함께 여행을 가게 될 사람
③ 소풍을 가게 될 날짜
④ 소년이 선생님의 말씀을 듣지 못한 이유
⑤ 소년이 여행을 가게 될 장소

1

M Hey, Mary, can you tell me ___________ ___________ ___________ ___________?
I need to get there right away.

W Yeah. You know where the post office is? Well, ___________ ___________ ___________ is
Hilton Road. Just turn left on Hilton Road and turn right ___________ ___________
___________ ___________. After the right turn, ___________ ___________ the highway. The mall
is on the other side. ___________ ___________ ___________ ___________?

M Yes, I got it. Thanks.

2

W Hi, Curtis, this is Jessica. I was calling ___________ ___________ ___________ about my party
next Thursday. My parents said ___________ ___________ ___________ five of my friends,
so I'm ___________ ___________. Oh, I'm sorry, but I have to go now. My mom ___________
___________ ___________ with something. Please ___________ ___________ ___________.

3

M Hello?

W Hey, Jacob. It's Jane.

M ___________ ___________ ___________, Jane? I thought we were going ___________ ___________
___________ ___________ this afternoon.

W I'm sorry, ___________ ___________ ___________ ___________. It's really noisy on this train.

M ___________ ___________ where you were .

W Oh. I went to visit my grandmother. She wanted to have lunch. ___________ ___________
___________. I'm so sorry.

M That's OK. ___________ ___________.

4

W Hello, this is Dr. Stevens' office. How can I ___________ ___________?

M Hi, this is Larry Butler. I need to schedule an appointment this week with Dr. Stevens.

W Yes, sir. Let's see. We have ___________ ___________ ___________. One is for 3:00 p.m. on
Tuesday. ___________ ___________ ___________ for 1:00 p.m. on Friday.

M Sorry. ___________ ___________ ___________ that again?

W You can come in at 3:00 p.m. on Tuesday or 1:00 p.m. on Friday.

M Well, Friday ___________ ___________ ___________ with me.

W Okay, sir.

5

M Good afternoon, ma'am. Where ___________ ___________ ___________ ___________ today?

W The First National Bank, please.

M I'm sorry, ___________ ___________ ___________ ___________. Where was that again?

W The First National Bank. And ___________ ___________.

M All right. I'll try. But there was ___________ ___________ ___________. We'll have to take

___________ ___________.

W Fine. Just get there ___________ ___________ ___________ possible, please.

6

M How ___________ ___________ ___________ the evening, Leslie?

W It's been really nice. ___________ ___________ a second. My phone is ___________ ___________.
I just got a message.

M ___________ ___________ ___________?

W I'm sorry, but ___________ ___________ ___________ now. That was my roommate. Our apart-
ment ___________ ___________ ___________. She just found out.

M Oh, I'm sorry. Of course ___________ ___________ ___________.

7

W Oh, it's so hard ___________ ___________ ___________ with so little money.

M Well, why don't you try ___________ ___________ ___________?

W Sorry. Would you ___________ ___________ ___________, please?

M A flea market. You know, it's where people ___________ ___________ ___________ things at
almost half price. You could get ___________ ___________ ___________ from one of those.

W Maybe. But I don't know where or ___________ ___________ ___________.

M I'll show you ___________ ___________ that can help you.

8

M Mr. Lawrence, I'm writing this e-mail ___________ ___________ ___________ today's
announcement. You told us when the school picnic would be. ___________ ___________
___________ ___________ again? I'm sorry, I didn't hear you. The student ___________
___________ ___________ kept whispering to me. I just ___________ ___________ ___________
___________ I can make it to the picnic. I might be going to Philadelphia ___________
___________ ___________ on that day. Thanks.

XI

HAVE YOU EVER SEEN IT?

경험 묻기

~해본 경험이 있으세요? / 없으세요?	Have you (ever) ~? / Haven't you (ever) ~?
~을 먹어본 경험이 있으세요?	Have you (ever) eaten ~? Have you (ever) tried to eat ~?

경험 유무 대답하기

네, 있어요.	Yes, I have.
아니요, 없어요.	No, I haven't.
~을 본 경험이 있어요. / ~을 먹어봤어요.	I have seen ~. / I have eaten ~.
~을 해 보았어요.	I have tried doing/to do ~.
~에 가본 경험이 없어요.	I haven't been to ~.

Words   *Vision*

appear	appearance	aliens	contact lenses	definitely
for sure	look at	notice	real	recognize

01 대화를 듣고, 남자의 친구를 골라 ✓ 표 하세요.

02 대화를 듣고, 두 사람이 각각 즐겨 하는 운동에 ✓ 표 하세요.

	Jill	Bryan
golf		
basketball		
soccer		

03 주어진 표현을 사용하여 대화를 완성하세요.

Have you ever tried	Yes, I have
I've also tried eating	No, I haven't

A ___________________ to eat a whole pizza at once?

B ________________. It made me really sick. ___________________ a whole chicken. Have you?

A ________________.

들려주는 내용을 잘 듣고 물음에 답하세요.

1 다음을 듣고, 남자가 말하고 있는 것이 무엇인지 고르세요.

① 산사태　　　　　② 우박　　　　　③ 토네이도
④ 화산폭발　　　　⑤ 눈보라

2 대화를 듣고, 여자가 취하고 있는 자세를 고르세요.

①　　　　②　　　　③　　　　④　　　　⑤

3 대화를 듣고, 여자의 직업을 고르세요.

① 가수　　　　② 교수　　　　③ 화가　　　　④ 시인　　　　⑤ 의사

4 대화를 듣고, 여자의 말에 이어질 남자의 응답으로 알맞은 것을 고르세요.

M

① Yes, they are fun to play with.
② That's what Mr. Green told me.
③ You can't talk to her anymore.
④ I've never spoken with him before.
⑤ No, his stories are all very interesting.

5 대화를 듣고, 여자가 남자에게 말을 건 이유를 고르세요.

① 남자친구에 대해 의논하기 위해서　② 조언을 구하기 위해서
③ 여행에 대해 불평하기 위해서　④ 남자를 여행에 초대하기 위해서
⑤ 호텔 가격을 비교하기 위해서

6 다음을 듣고, 여자의 꿈이 무엇인지 고르세요.

① 음악 선생님이 되는 것
② TV 프로그램에 출연하는 것
③ 돈을 많이 벌어 부자가 되는 것
④ 세계적으로 유명한 배우가 되는 것
⑤ 예술대학에 입학하는 것

7 대화를 듣고, 남자의 심정으로 알맞은 것을 고르세요.

①  ②  ③  ④  ⑤ 

8 대화를 듣고, 대화의 상황을 가장 잘 설명한 것을 고르세요.

① 두 사람은 데이트 중이다.
② 여자는 짝사랑 중이다.
③ 남자는 여자친구와 헤어졌다.
④ 남자는 여자를 짝사랑하고 있다.
⑤ 두 사람은 헤어지고 싶어한다.

다음을 듣고 빈칸에 들어갈 알맞은 말을 쓰세요.

1

M ____________ ____________ ____________ ____________ one of these? They are like clouds, but they reach from the sky to the ground. They also __________ __________ very quickly. This is because dangerous wind __________ __________ __________ is causing them. They can destroy __________ __________ __________. If you see one, you are __________ __________ __________. Hide, and get away from any windows immediately!

2

M Hey, Karen. __________ __________ __________ __________ this yoga pose before?

W Let's see. Yes, I have. __________ __________ __________ a little difficult at first.

M How do you do it?

W Well, the first thing you do is __________ __________ __________ together, like this. Then you raise __________ __________ __________ __________ over your head. Finally, stand on just your right leg. Then bring __________ __________ __________ __________ to your right knee.

M Ah, I think I got it now. Thanks.

3

M __________ __________ __________ __________ a lot of time and care into a creative project, Penny?

W __________, __________ __________. I recently finished a painting. __________ __________ __________ on it for months now.

M You must really enjoy __________ __________.

W I do. It __________ __________ __________. And it lets me use my imagination.

4

W Mr. Green sure is amazing!

M Uh, who is Mr. Green?

W He works at the security office. He's __________ __________ __________ __________ as my grandfather. And he has some __________ __________ __________!

M Really? Like what?

W Well, __________ __________ __________ both the Korean and Vietnam Wars. He was also a police officer in New York. __________ __________ __________ __________ with him?

5

W Devon, __________ __________ on lots of vacations, right?

M Yeah, I guess so.

Dictation

W Have you ever gone ______________ ______________ ______________ ______________ before?

M Yes, I have. A few times. ______________ ______________ ______________ ______________ ?

W Well, I am thinking of going on one with my parents. ______________ ______________ ______________ the price?

M I think so. You ______________ ______________ ______________ all kinds of nice islands and beaches. You can also do all kinds ______________ ______________ ______________ on the ship itself. They're ______________ ______________ ______________ most hotels!

W Really? That's interesting. Thank you.

6

W Hey, Shelly. I haven't ______________ ______________ ______________ in a while. I was just sending this e-mail to see ______________ ______________ ______________ ______________ . Also, I posted a link to the Fine Arts Academy of Hartford on here. ______________ ______________ ______________ ______________ of this place? It teaches people ______________ ______________ ______________ , act, dance, and play music! You know ______________ ______________ ______________ is to appear on the show *American Idol* someday. Maybe these people ______________ ______________ ______________ with that.

7

W Hey, Billy. I have a question.

M What is it?

W Have you ever seen ______________ ______________ ______________ ?

M No, I haven't. I thought ______________ ______________ ______________ . But that was back when ______________ ______________ ______________ ______________ . It was just a plane.

W Oh. Do you think ______________ ______________ ______________ ?

M I really don't know.

W What if they are real? Would you ______________ ______________ ?

M Look, ______________ ______________ ______________ right now. Can we talk about this later?

8

M Wendy, I have a problem.

W What is it?

M Well, have you ever ______________ ______________ ______________ with someone who didn't love you?

W Yes, I have. It ______________ ______________ ______________ . Is that what's wrong?

M Yeah. There's this girl in my chemistry class ______________ ______________ ______________ . But I don't think she even ______________ ______________ . I want to ask her out, but I'm too nervous!

W Gee, that's rough. But you should ______________ ______________ ______________ . Otherwise, you'll never know for sure!

XII CHEER UP!

소망하기/기원하기

당신이 잘했으면 좋겠어요.	I hope you do well. / I wish you well.
당신이 빨리 회복되었으면 좋겠어요.	I hope you get well soon.
모든 것이 잘 풀렸으면 좋겠어요.	I hope everything goes well.
행운을 빌어요.	Good luck (to you). / God bless you.
	I'll keep my fingers crossed for you.

격려하기

기운내세요.	Cheer up.
다음엔 더 잘할 거에요.	You'll do better next time.
긍정적으로 생각하세요.	Look on the bright side.

Words   *Health*

- blood pressure
- dangerous
- get sick
- healthy
- heart attack
- maintain
- recover
- risk
- test result
- treat
- turn out

01 대화를 듣고, 두 사람이 만난 장소를 골라 ✓ 표 하세요.

02 대화를 듣고, 여자가 경연에 참가하려고 하는 이유를 골라 ✓ 표 하세요.

a 유명한 가수가 되고 싶어서

b 다른 연예인들을 만나보고 싶어서

c 상금을 타고 싶어서

03 주어진 표현을 사용하여 대화를 완성하세요.

You'll do better	Cheer up
Good luck on	I wish you well, too

A _________________ today's English test.

B Thanks. _____________________.

[*two hours later*]

A How was your test?

B I think I failed again.

A ________________. You can take it next month. _______________ next time.

들려주는 내용을 잘 듣고 물음에 답하세요.

1 다음 그림의 상황에 맞는 대화를 고르세요.

①   ②   ③   ④   ⑤

2 다음을 듣고, 여자가 경기를 보러 가지 <u>못하는</u> 이유를 고르세요.

① 타고 갈 차량이 마땅치 않아서   ② 중요한 회의에 참석해야 해서

③ 다른 사람들과의 선약이 있어서   ④ 집안 행사가 있어서

⑤ 아르바이트를 해야 해서

3 대화를 듣고, 여자의 마지막 말의 의도를 고르세요.

① 불평   ② 동의   ③ 기원   ④ 사과   ⑤ 부탁

4 대화를 듣고, 일치하지 <u>않는</u> 내용을 고르세요.

① 여자는 새로운 록 밴드를 결성했다.

② 여자의 밴드는 해체되었다.

③ 여자는 록 밴드의 멤버였다.

④ 여자의 밴드에는 두 명의 기타리스트가 있었다.

⑤ 여자는 예전 멤버들과 함께 공연을 하고 싶어한다.

5 대화를 듣고, 여자가 병원을 다녀온 이유를 고르세요.

① 의사에게 진찰을 받으려고
② 엄마가 병원에 입원해 계셔서
③ 수술 예약을 하려고
④ 엄마가 병원에 근무를 하고 있어서
⑤ 친척 병문안을 가려고

6 다음을 듣고, 남자가 전하고자 하는 의미로 알맞은 것을 고르세요.

① You need to work harder.
② I should be a famous actor.
③ Just give up your silly dreams.
④ I'll keep my fingers crossed for you.
⑤ I'm happy you got the part.

7 대화를 듣고, 남자의 직업이 무엇인지 고르세요.

① ② ③ ④ ⑤

8 대화를 듣고, 새로운 시장에 대한 여자의 의견으로 알맞은 것을 고르세요.

① He was a nice businessman.
② He is too nice.
③ He will make the town better.
④ He will be a bad mayor.
⑤ He is a good speaker.

다음을 듣고 빈칸에 들어갈 알맞은 말을 쓰세요.

1

① M I hope __________ __________ __________ on this test.
  W Thanks. I wish __________ __________, too.

② M I hope __________ __________ __________ in your new life together.
  W Thanks, Uncle Bob! And __________ __________ __________ to the wedding.

③ M Well, I'm going to __________ __________ __________ my best swimming time.
  W I'll keep __________ __________ __________ for you.

④ M That book I wanted wasn't at the bookstore.
  W __________ __________. Here, you can borrow my copy.

⑤ M __________ __________. You'll need it on this slope.
  W Yeah. I'm not sure I can ski this well.

2

W Dear Max,
  I heard that __________ __________ __________ made it to the championship game next weekend. That's incredible! __________ __________! I wish I could fly out there to see you. Unfortunately, I have __________ __________ __________ __________ next weekend, so I can't. Still, I'll be __________ __________ __________. Take care!
  Sincerely,
  Aunt Glenda

3

M Hey, Patty. __________ __________ __________?
W I'm doing okay. __________ __________ __________ __________, Steven?
M Alright. I'm actually preparing to take __________ __________ __________ tomorrow.
W Really? __________ __________ __________ where you want to go to school?
M Not really. I want to see __________ __________ __________ on the test first before I start __________ __________.
W Well, good luck __________ __________ __________.

4

W This is just great.
M __________ __________, Claudia?
W The two guitarists in my rock band don't want __________ __________ __________ anymore. So our band __________ __________ __________.
M Oh, too bad. But look __________ __________ __________ __________. Now you can start your own band. You've always wanted to do that, right?

W Yeah. I still liked playing __________ __________ _________, though.

M Well, maybe __________ __________ _________ will still play with you.

5

M You look __________ __________ _________, Martha. What's the matter?

W I just got back from visiting my mom __________ __________ _________.

M Oh, no! Is she okay?

W She's recovering from __________ __________ _________. She's doing better. But she's

__________ __________ _________.

M I'm sorry to hear that. I hope she __________ __________ _________.

6

M Hey, Sara. I heard that you're going to audition __________ __________ _________ in a
movie. I know that you've wanted __________ __________ __________ _________ for a
long time. This will be a good chance for you. I've always __________ _________, and I
know you'll do great __________ __________ _________.

7

W So, how did my test results __________ _________?

M They're okay, but your blood pressure is __________ __________ _________, Martha. You
need to __________ __________ _________ before it becomes dangerous.

W Oh, this is terrible. I don't want __________ __________ _________!

M __________ _________. Just eat healthy foods and exercise more. __________ __________
_________ your blood pressure.

W Okay. Thanks.

8

M Well, it looks like Jack Pearson is going to be ______ __________ __________ _________.

W I can't believe he won the election.

M Well, he might not be that bad.

W What are you talking about? He didn't know __________ __________ _________ his own
company. How well can he run the town? Things __________ __________ _________.

M Look on the bright side. __________ _________ to a new town in a few months. You
won't have to __________ __________ _________.

W Yeah, I guess you're right.

Memo

Memo

Memo

Answer & Script

센치한 Listening 길들이기

감성 맞춤 내신 공략

내신 만점을 향한 중등 영어 듣기 기본서

- 최신 개정 교육과정 분석 및 필수 의사소통 기능 수록
- 실제 영어 듣기평가와 가장 가까운 문제 유형 및 소재 제시
- 효과적인 1일 학습량 제시
- 다시 한 번 확인하는 Dictation 코너
- 시·도 교육청 듣기평가 대비 실전 모의고사 3회 수록

도약 **2**

센치한 Listening 길들이기

감성 맞춤 내신 공략

도약 2

woongjin compass

UNIT 1 MAY I HAVE THIS?

⚙ Check Up

01 b **02** 1. F 2. T

03 A Uncle Tom, <u>Can I go and take</u> some pictures of your house? It's for my art class.
 B <u>Feel free to do so.</u>
 A Oh, thank you. <u>Let me know</u> when I can visit you. Can I visit you at 2 p.m.?
 B That's <u>fine with me.</u>

Check Up Scripts

01

M I heard that your father is having problems with his car.

W Yeah. It seems like there's something wrong with the engine. It doesn't always run when he starts the car.

M Hmm. Let me know if I can help him with it. I'm pretty good with auto repair.

W That's good. You might save him some money on repairs.

남 너희 아버지 차에 문제가 생겼다고 들었어.

여 맞아요. 엔진에 문제가 있는 것 같아요. 시동을 걸려고 해도 계속 엔진이 돌아가지를 않아요.

남 흠. 내가 도울 수 있으면 말해 주렴. 난 자동차 수리를 꽤 잘하거든.

여 잘됐네요. 저희 아빠가 수리하는 비용을 절약 할 수 있겠어요.

Vocabulary	problem 문제　engine 엔진　run 작동하다　start the car 시동을 걸다　auto repair 자동차 수리

02

W Dad, may I have a party this weekend? I promise I'll only invite a few friends.

M Yes, you may have a party this weekend. But I want you to clean up your room first.

W But it is clean!

M No, it's not. And I don't want visitors to see such a dirty room.

여 아빠, 이번 주말에 파티 열어도 되요? 친구들은 조금만 초대한다고 약속할게요.

남 좋아. 주말에 파티를 열어도 좋다. 하지만 네 방을 먼저 청소했으면 좋겠구나.

여 하지만 방은 깨끗해요!

남 아니, 그렇지 않아. 나는 손님들이 그런 더러운 방을 보는 것을 원치 않는단다.

Vocabulary	promise 약속하다　invite 초대하다　clean up 청소하다　visitor 손님

03

A Uncle Tom. Can I go and take some pictures of your house? It's for my art class.

B Feel free to do so.

A Oh, thank you. Let me know when I can visit you. Can I visit you at 2 p.m.?

B That's fine with me.

A Tom 삼촌. 삼촌 집 사진을 찍으러 가도 될까요? 제 미술수업 때문에 그래요.

B 마음대로 하거라.

A 오. 고마워요. 언제 방문하면 될지 알려주세요. 오후 2시에 가면 될까요?

B 그러렴.

Actual Test   1 ③   2 ⑤   3 ②   4 ①   5 ③   6 ②   7 ⑤   8 ③ | p.08

1

① **M** May I pet the dog, Mom?

    W No, you may not. It might be dangerous.

② **M** Ms. Cooper, may I please sit closer to the chalkboard? I'm having trouble seeing it.

    W Yes, you may sit closer.

③ **M** Can I use your computer for a second? I need to check my e-mail.

    W Feel free to use my computer.

④ **W** Can I use your cell phone for a minute?

    M Sure, go ahead.

⑤ **W** Please let me know if I can borrow your science book tonight.

    M Sure, go ahead. I don't need to study it today.

① 남 애완동물 길러도 될까요, 엄마?

    여 아니, 안 된단다. 위험할 수 있어.

② 남 Cooper 선생님, 칠판 가까이에 앉아도 될까요? 잘 안보여서요.

    여 그래, 가까이 앉으렴.

③ 남 잠시 네 컴퓨터 좀 써도 될까? 이메일을 확인해야 되거든.

    여 마음대로 사용해도 좋아.

④ 여 네 휴대폰 좀 써도 될까?

    남 물론이지.

⑤ 여 오늘 저녁에 네 과학 책을 빌릴 수 있는지 알려줘.

    남 그렇게 해. 난 오늘은 그것을 공부할 필요가 없어.

2

M Mom, can I miss class today?

W I'm afraid you can't. Is something troubling you?

M It's just… I hate going to school every day. It's so boring. I don't understand the lessons. I don't know what to do.

W David, thank you for telling me that. I'll help you with your lessons. Let's study them together, starting today.

남 엄마, 오늘 결석해도 될까요?

여 미안하지만 안 된다. 무슨 일 있니?

남 그게… 전 매일 학교에 가는 것이 싫어요. 너무 지루해요. 수업도 이해가 안돼요. 무엇을 해야 할지 모르겠어요.

여 David, 나에게 말해줘서 고맙구나. 내가 너의 공부를 도와줄게. 오늘부터 함께 공부하자꾸나.

3

W Dad, may I take this cat home with me?

M No, you may not. We only came in here for some more goldfish.

W But he's so cute! I promise I'll take good care of him.

M You can talk to your mother about it later. But we're only buying some more goldfish today.

여	아빠, 이 고양이를 집에 데려가도 될까요?
남	아니, 그럼 안돼. 우리는 단지 금붕어 몇 마리를 더 사기 위해 이곳에 온 거잖니.
여	하지만, 그가 너무 귀여워요! 제가 잘 돌봐줄게요.
남	네 엄마하고 나중에 이야기를 해보려무나. 우리는 오늘 금붕어 몇 마리만 살 거란다.

| Vocabulary | gold fish 금붕어   promise 약속하다   take care of 돌보다 |

4

[The answering machine beeps.]

W Hi, it's me, honey. I will be home a little bit later this evening. I was wondering what you wanted to do for dinner. Let me know if I should pick up something to eat for you. I can get a pizza or something else on my way home, if you'd like. Talk to you later. Love you!

[자동응답기 소리]

여 안녕, 엄마다. 얘야. 오늘 저녁에 집에 조금 늦을 것 같아. 저녁으로 뭘 했으면 좋을지 싶구나. 너를 위해 먹을거리를 사가야 할 지 말해주렴. 원한다면, 집으로 가는 길에 피자나 다른 것을 사갈게. 나중에 얘기하자. 사랑한다!

| Vocabulary | wonder 궁금하다   a little bit 조금   pick up 사다   on one's way 가는 길에 |

5

M Ellen, can I borrow your math book? I left mine at the school.

W Feel free to use it. I just need it back by tomorrow morning.

M Thanks. I have a big test tomorrow. To tell you the truth, I'm a little nervous.

W What is your test going to be about?

M Some geometry formulas.

W Well, I can help you, if you want. I am pretty good at that stuff.

M Then can you see me tonight?

남 Ellen, 수학 책 좀 빌려줄래? 내 책을 학교에 놓고 왔어.

여 마음대로 봐. 내일 아침까지만 돌려주면 돼.

남 고마워. 나 내일 중요한 시험이 있어. 사실, 난 좀 걱정이 돼.

여 무엇에 관한 시험이니?

남 기하학 공식이야.

여 음, 네가 원한다면 내가 도와줄 수 있어. 내가 그걸 좀 잘 하거든.

남 그럼 오늘 밤에 볼 수 있니?

| Vocabulary | truth 사실   nervous 걱정하는   geometry 기하학   formula 공식   good at ~을 잘하다 |

M Let me tell you about space camp. It's the most fun summer camp in the country! Here, you learn all about space, planets, and rocket ships! You can talk to people who have visited space! They'll tell you what it's like to walk on the moon. You can even play special video games about space travel. So join us today!

남 여러분에게 우주캠프에 대해 말씀 드리겠습니다. 이것은 국내에서 가장 재미있는 여름 캠프입니다! 이곳에서 여러분은 우주와, 행성 그리고 우주 항공기에 대해 배울 수 있습니다! 여러분은 우주에 다녀온 사람들과 이야기를 나눌 수도 있습니다! 그들은 여러분에게 달 위를 걷는 것이 어떠한지 알려드릴 것입니다. 여러분은 우주 여행과 관련된 특별한 비디오 게임도 즐기실 수 있습니다. 그러니 오늘 신청하세요!

Vocabulary	space camp 우주캠프　　planet 행성　　rocket ship 로켓선, 우주 항공기

M Janice, is there going to be a club meeting on Thursday?

W Yeah. It's going to be about the new computers. It will last from 11 to 1.

M Great. May I make a short presentation during the meeting? I'll show the new members how to use some programs on the new computers.

W Yes, you may do a presentation. In fact, I think that's a good idea.

M Cool. Oh, and I heard we were ordering lunch. How much money should we bring for the lunch order?

W Please bring $7. That should cover everything.

남 Janice, 목요일에 동아리 모임이 있니?

여 응. 새로운 컴퓨터에 대한 거야. 11시부터 1시까지 진행될 거야.

남 잘됐네. 회의시간에 간단한 프레젠테이션을 해도 될까? 신입 회원들에게 새로운 컴퓨터에 깔려 있는 몇몇 프로그램에 대한 사용법을 보여주려고.

여 그래. 프레젠테이션을 해. 사실, 난 좋은 생각인 것 같아.

남 좋아. 아, 그리고 점심을 주문한다고 들었는데. 점심을 주문하려면 얼마를 가져와야 하는 거야?

여 7달러를 가져오면 돼. 그걸로 모든 것이 해결 될 거야.

Vocabulary	meeting 모임, 회의　　last 지속하다　　presentation 발표, 프레젠테이션　　during ~동안에　　in fact 사실 order 주문하다　　bring 가져오다, 지참하다

M Lisa, can I speak with you a minute?

W Sure, what is it?

M I had a little chat with Mr. Murphy yesterday afternoon.

W What did he tell you?

남 Lisa, 얘기 좀 할 수 있을까?

여 물론이지요, 무슨 일이세요?

남 어제 오후에 Murphy씨하고 이야기를 했단다.

여 그가 뭐라고 했는데요?

M He said that you often <u>fall</u> <u>asleep</u> in his class.

W I'm sorry, Dad. I try to stay awake, but I <u>feel</u> <u>so</u> <u>tired</u> all the time.

M Well, that is not <u>a</u> <u>good</u> excuse. Every student has to study at school.

W I'm so sorry.

남 네가 그의 수업시간에 종종 잠을 잔다고 하더구나.

여 죄송해요, 아빠. 저는 깨어있으려고 하는데, 항상 너무 피곤해요.

남 음, 그건 좋은 변명이 아니란다. 모든 학생들은 학교에서 공부를 해야 해.

여 정말 죄송해요.

| Vocabulary | fall asleep 잠들다 | stay awake 깨어있다 | excuse 변명 |

UNIT II WHO'S CALLING?

☆ Check Up

01 c **02** she dialed the wrong number.

03 A Hello. <u>Is Karen there?</u>

B May I ask <u>who's calling</u>, please?

A <u>This is her classmate</u>, Timothy.

B <u>Hold on, I'll get</u> her for you.

A Thank you.

Check Up Scripts

01

[The telephone rings.]

M Hello, is Sandra there?

W It's me. Who's calling?

M Oh, It's Jason. Listen. I lost my pet dog just a while ago. Can you help me look for him?

W OK. What does it look like?

M He is white and has brown dots.

W All right. I will call you if I find him.

M Thank you!

[전화벨 소리]

남 여보세요, Sandra 있나요?

여 저에요. 누구세요?

남 오, Jason이야. 들어봐. 내가 방금 전에 내 애완견을 잃어버렸어. 그를 찾도록 도와줄 수 있니?

여 알겠어. 그는 어떻게 생겼니?

남 하얀색이고 갈색 점들이 있어.

여 좋아. 그를 찾게 되면 바로 전화할게.

남 고마워!

Vocabulary	a while ago 조금 전에 look for 찾다 look like ~처럼 생기다 dot 점

02

[The telephone rings.]

M Hello?

W Hi, this is Allison Smith with Jackson Auto Repair. Is Mr. Allan Buford there?

M Sorry. You've got the wrong number.

W Wait. Is this 555-6432?

M Oh, no. This is 555-6765.

W I'm very sorry, sir. It's my mistake.

M No problem.

[전화벨 소리]

남 여보세요?

여 안녕하세요, Jackson 정비소의 Allison Smith입니다. Allan Buford씨 계신가요?

남 죄송합니다. 전화를 잘못 거신 것 같아요.

여 잠시만요. 555-6432 아닌가요?

남 오, 아니에요. 여기는 555-6765에요.

여 정말 죄송합니다. 제 실수에요.

남 괜찮습니다.

Vocabulary	auto repair 자동차 정비소 mistake 실수 hang up 전화를 끊다

03

A Hello. Is Karen there?

B May I ask who's calling, please?

A This is her classmate, Timothy.

B Hold on, I'll get her for you.

A Thank you.

A 여보세요. Karen 있나요?

B 전화하신 분은 누구시죠?

A 반 친구인 Timothy라고 합니다.

B 기다리세요, 그녀를 바꿔드릴게요.

A 감사합니다.

Vocabulary	hold on 기다리다

Actual Test   1 ②   2 ④   3 ③   4 ④   5 ②   6 ③   7 ④   8 ① | p.14

[The telephone rings.]

M Hello, is this the First National Bank?

W Yes, it is. How can I help you, sir?

M I want to know where you're located. My Internet is down, so I can't look up directions there.

W No problem, sir. Drive east on Elm Street. Turn right onto Carter Avenue, and then take your first left.

M So the bank will be on that street, then?

W Yes, sir. It will be the second building on the left.

[전화벨 소리]

남 여보세요, First 국립은행인가요?

여 네, 맞습니다. 무엇을 도와드릴까요, 손님?

남 그 곳이 어디에 위치에 있는지를 알고 싶어요. 제 인터넷이 연결이 안돼서, 그쪽으로 가는 길을 찾아볼 수가 없어요.

여 문제 없습니다, 손님. Elm 거리에서 동쪽으로 가세요. Carter 거리 쪽으로 우회전을 하시고 나서 첫 번째로 나오는 길에서 좌회전 하세요.

남 그럼 은행이 그 거리에 있다는 말씀이신가요?

여 그렇습니다, 손님. 왼쪽에 있는 두 번째 건물입니다.

Vocabulary	national bank 국립은행 locate 위치하다 down (연결이) 끊어지다 look up (컴퓨터 등으로 정보를) 검색하다
	direction 방향, 위치 avenue 거리, -가 street 거리, 도로

[The answering machine beeps.]

W Hi, this is Clara. You've reached my answering machine. Sorry, I can't come to the phone right now. I'm on vacation in Europe. I'll be back next Friday. Please leave your name and number. I'll contact you after I get back. You can send me messages through e-mail, though. Thanks, and talk to you later!

[자동응답기 소리]

여 안녕하세요, 저는 Clara입니다. 당신은 제 자동응답기로 연락하셨습니다. 죄송하지만 저는 지금 전화를 받을 수가 없습니다. 저는 유럽에서 휴가 중입니다. 저는 다음주 금요일에 돌아올 겁니다. 당신의 이름과 전화번호를 남겨주세요. 돌아오면 연락을 드리겠습니다. 이메일로 연락을 주셔도 됩니다. 감사하고, 다음에 연락 합시다!

3

[The telephone rings.]

M Hello. I need to speak with Charlie. <u>Is he</u> <u>available</u>?

W <u>Who's calling</u>, please?

M This is Bob. I have the same chemistry class as Charlie. <u>I missed</u> yesterday's class and I wanted to <u>get</u> some notes from him tomorrow.

W Hold on, please. <u>I'll get</u> him.

[전화벨 소리]

남 여보세요. Charlie와 통화하고 싶은데요. 통화가 가능한가요?

여 전화하신 분은 누구시죠?

남 Bob이라고 해요. Charlie와 같은 화학 수업을 듣고 있어요. 제가 어제 수업에 참석을 못해서 내일 그에게서 공책을 좀 빌리고 싶어요.

여 잠시만 기다리세요. 바꿔드릴게요.

4

[The telephone rings.]

M Hello, this is Mike Sanders. Is Dr. Stephens available?

W Dr. Stephens? I'm sorry, but he just stepped out. Would you like to <u>leave a</u> <u>message</u>?

M Yes, please. I bought <u>a couple of cats</u> two days ago. Then <u>a red rash</u> broke out and my skin started <u>to get itchy</u>. I don't know what to do.

W Oh, that must be hard for you. I'll tell him <u>when</u> he <u>gets back</u>.

M Thank you.

[전화벨 소리]

남 여보세요, Mike Sanders라고 하는데요. Stephens 선생님 계신가요?

여 Stephens선생님이요? 죄송하지만, 방금 외출하셨어요. 메시지를 남기시겠어요?

남 네, 그럴게요. 제가 이틀 전에 고양이 두 마리를 샀어요. 그런데 갑자기 빨간 두드러기가 생기면서 제 피부가 가렵기 시작했어요. 어떻게 해야 할지 모르겠어요.

여 오, 괴로우시겠네요. 그가 돌아오면 전해드릴게요.

남 고맙습니다.

5

[The answering machine beeps.]

W Hello, Mr. Walker. <u>This is</u> your son's English teacher, Ms. Harris. <u>I'm calling</u> because your son has missed <u>some of my classes</u> recently. He has not attended class <u>in three days</u>. I have not been able <u>to talk to him</u> about this. I

[자동응답기 소리]

여 안녕하세요, Walker씨. 저는 아드님의 영어 선생님인 Harris라고 합니다. 최근 댁의 아드님이 제 수업의 일부를 참석하지 않아서 전화를 드립니다. 사흘이나 수업을 듣지 않았습니다. 그와 이것에 대해 이야기를 나누지 못했어요. 제 생각에는 결석에 관한 상담을 좀 해야 할 것 같아요. 제

think we need to have a meeting <u>about these</u> <u>absences</u>. Please <u>call me back</u> at my office at 834-0987.

교무실 전화인 834–0987로 전화 좀 부탁 드리겠습니다.

[The telephone rings.]

M Hello, I'm <u>with</u> Johnson Cosmetics. We're calling some customers <u>for a quick</u> <u>survey</u>. It will only take a moment.

W OK.

M Great. <u>May I ask</u> how old you are?

W 15.

M Uh-huh. And how often do you <u>buy</u> <u>our products</u>?

W Every few months.

M OK. And have you <u>had any problems</u> with these products?

W No. They were all fine.

M Great. That's <u>all I needed</u>. Thank you for your time.

[전화벨 소리]

남 여보세요, Johnson 화장품 업체입니다. 저희는 간단한 설문조사를 위해 몇몇 고객 분들께 전화를 하고 있습니다. 시간은 얼마 걸리지 않을 거에요.

여 알겠어요.

남 좋습니다. 연령을 여쭤봐도 될까요?

여 15살이에요.

남 네. 그럼 얼마나 자주 저희 제품을 구매하시나요?

여 몇 달에 한 번씩이요.

남 알겠습니다. 그럼 저희 제품에 문제가 있었던 적이 있으세요?

여 아니요. 다 괜찮았어요.

남 좋아요. 이제 다 됐습니다. 시간을 내 주셔서 감사합니다.

[The telephone rings.]

W Hello, is Ms. Carol Summers there?

M Who's <u>calling</u>, please?

W This is Rachel at Stoker's Pharmacy.

M Oh. Well, Carol <u>isn't here right now</u>. This is her dad. Can I <u>take a message</u> for her?

W Yes, Mr. Summers. Her medicine is ready <u>to pick up</u>. I'm calling to let her know.

M Great, I'll <u>tell her</u> when she gets back. Thank you.

[전화벨 소리]

여 여보세요, Carol Summers양 계신가요?

남 누구시죠?

여 Stockers 약국의 Rachel이라고 합니다.

남 오. Carol은 지금 없습니다. 저는 그녀의 아버지에요. 메시지를 전해드릴까요?

여 네, Summers씨. 그녀의 약을 가지러 오셔도 됩니다. 그녀에게 알려 드리려고 전화 드렸어요.

남 잘됐군요, 그녀가 돌아오면 전해줄게요. 고맙습니다.

[The telephone rings.]

M Hello?

W Hi, Carlton. It's Jane. <u>Are you</u> free tonight?
I got <u>free</u> <u>movie</u> <u>tickets</u>.

M I'm sorry, but I have an important
presentation tomorrow.

W Oh. Well, what about <u>your</u> <u>roommate</u>,
Heath? <u>Is he around</u>?

M Yes, he <u>just</u> <u>came</u> <u>in</u>.

W Great! Can I talk to him?

Vocabulary	free 한가한, 공짜의

[전화벨 소리]

남 여보세요?

여 안녕. Carlton. 나 Jane이야. 오늘 저녁에 시간 괜찮니? 나에게 공짜 영화 표가 생겼거든.

남 미안하지만. 나는 내일 중요한 발표가 있어.

여 오. 그럼. 네 룸메이트인 Heath는? 그가 있니?

남 응. 방금 들어왔어.

여 잘됐다! 그와 통화할 수 있을까?

UNIT III I CAN'T WAIT!

✿ Check Up

01 b **02** 1. buy 2. stylish

03 A I'm looking forward to the next *Harry Potter* book.

B Me, too. I can't wait to read it.

A I'm also planning to go to see a movie of it next month.

B It sounds good. I hope to go, too.

Check Up Scripts

01

M Do you have any plans for the weekend, Lucy?

W I'm planning to visit my grandmother. It's been a while since I last saw her.

M Cool. What's she like?

W Well, she's got long blonde hair, and she wears these really thick glasses. She's always nice to me, too.

남 주말에 무슨 계획 있니, Lucy?

여 난 할머니를 뵈러 갈 거야. 그녀를 오랫동안 뵙지 못했거든.

남 좋겠다. 그녀는 어떻게 생기셨니?

여 음. 그녀는 긴 금발머리를 하고 있고, 굉장히 두꺼운 안경을 착용하셔. 그녀는 나에게 언제나 친절하셔.

Vocabulary	grandmother 할머니 blonde 금발의 wear 착용하다, 쓰다

02

M Linda, can I ask you for a favor?

W Sure, Rick. What is it?

M Well, I hope to buy a couch next week when I get paid. But I don't want to get some regular old couch. I want something stylish. Could you help me shop for one?

W Yeah, I could do that.

남 Linda, 부탁 좀 해도 될까?

여 물론이지, Rick. 뭔데?

남 음. 월급을 받으면 다음주에 소파를 하나 사고 싶어. 그런데 나는 평범하고 오래된 소파를 사고 싶지는 않아. 나는 멋진 것으로 사고 싶어. 내가 쇼핑하는 것을 좀 도와주겠니?

여 응, 그렇게 할게.

Vocabulary	favor 부탁 couch 소파 get paid 돈을 받다 regular 평범한 stylish 멋진 shop (가게에서 물건을) 사다, 쇼핑하다

03

A I'm looking forward to the next *Harry Potter* book.

B Me, too. I can't wait to read it.

A I'm also planning to go to see a movie of it next month.

B It sounds good. I hope to go, too.

A 나는 「해리포터」의 다음 편을 기대하고 있어.

B 나도야. 빨리 읽고 싶어.

A 나는 다음 달에 영화로도 보러 갈 거야.

B 재미있겠다. 나도 가고 싶어.

Vocabulary	look forward to ~하는 것을 고대하다

1

① **W** I want to catch the next train to the downtown marketplace.

  M Well, it won't be here for another 10 minutes.

② **M** Are you ready for next week?

  W Yeah. I'm looking forward to that fishing trip.

③ **M** I plan to do some surfing at the beach on Sunday. Want to come?

  W Sorry. I have other plans.

④ **M** Would you like to go river rafting this weekend?

  W Sure. I hope to see some of the beautiful countryside.

⑤ **W** I'm planning to play tennis tomorrow. Care to join?

  M Sorry, I can't. I have to finish some work.

① 여 저는 시내에 있는 장터에 가는 다음 기차를 타고 싶어요.

  남 음, 기차는 10분 더 기다려야 해요.

② 남 너 다음 주를 위한 준비 됐니?

  여 응. 나는 낚시 여행이 너무 기대돼.

③ 남 나는 일요일에 해변에서 서핑을 하려고 해. 같이 갈래?

  여 미안해. 나 다른 계획이 있어.

④ 남 이번 주말에 강 래프팅 가지 않을래?

  여 물론이야. 나는 아름다운 시골모습을 보고 싶어.

⑤ 여 나 내일 테니스 치러 갈 거야. 너도 갈래?

  남 미안하지만 난 안돼. 끝내야 할 일이 있어서.

Vocabulary	catch (기차 등을 타기 위해) 잡다 downtown 시내 marketplace 장터, 시장 surfing 서핑 rafting 래프팅
	countryside 시골

2

  W Good morning, Todd. Did you want to speak to me?

  M Yes, Ms. Hoover. I've decided to enter that essay contest next month. I'd like to win the prize. But I don't know what to write about.

  W Well, you should write about your interests. What is your favorite subject?

  M Hmm. Probably art.

  W Okay. Then just find a way to fit that into an essay. That's how you produce good writing.

  M Thanks. I'll try doing that.

  여 좋은 아침이구나, Todd. 나와 얘기하고 싶어했니?

  남 네, Hoover선생님. 전 다음 달에 그 백일장에 참가하려고 해요. 저는 상을 받고 싶어요. 하지만 무엇에 대해 써야 할지 모르겠어요.

  여 음. 넌 네가 흥미로워하는 것에 대해 쓰면 돼. 네가 좋아하는 과목이 무엇이니?

  남 흠. 아마도 미술이요.

  여 좋아. 그렇다면 그것을 글에 적용시킬 방법을 찾아보렴. 그것이 좋은 글을 쓰는 방법이야.

  남 고맙습니다. 그렇게 해보도록 할게요.

Vocabulary	enter 참가하다 contest 경합, 대회 win the prize 우승하다, 상을 타다 interest 관심사 favorite 가장 좋아하는
	subject 과목 probably 아마도 fit A into B A를 B에 맞추다 produce 만들다 proper 적당한, 알맞은

3

W Well, it looks like another boring weekend for me.

M Really? You don't have any plans?

W No. I want to get out and do something else.

M Well, I'm planning to go hiking this Sunday. You're welcome to join us if you like.

W Who are you going with?

M My roommates, Timmy and Mike.

W Then can my sister join, too?

M Sure, why not? I can't wait!

여 음. 난 또 지루한 주말을 보내게 될 것 같아.

남 정말? 너 아무런 계획이 없니?

여 없어. 나는 외출을 해서 무언가 다른 것을 하고 싶어.

남 음. 난 이번 주 일요일에 하이킹을 가려고 하거든. 원한다면 우리와 함께 가도 좋아.

여 누구와 함께 가는데?

남 내 룸메이트인 Timmy와 Mike와 갈 거야.

여 그럼 내 여동생도 함께 가도 될까?

남 물론이지. 왜 안되겠어? 너무 기대된다!

Vocabulary	get out 나가다 welcome 환영 받는 join 함께하다

4

W I'm looking forward to this Saturday. A lot of my friends are coming to see me. We're going to play lots of games, watch movies, and just have fun. I'll be getting a lot of presents, too. It's to celebrate my getting older. I always love these occasions. It's just too bad they only happen once a year.

여 난 이번 주 토요일을 고대하고 있습니다. 많은 내 친구들이 나를 보러 올겁니다. 우리는 여러 게임을 할 것이고, 영화도 보고, 재미있게 놀겁니다. 나는 많은 선물도 받을 거예요. 그것은 내가 나이를 먹는 것을 기념하기 위한 것입니다. 나는 언제나 이러한 행사들을 좋아합니다. 그 행사들이 일년에 한 번씩만 있다는 것이 아쉬울 뿐입니다.

Vocabulary	present 선물 celebrate 기념하다 occasion 행사 happen 있다, 발생하다

5

M My name is Harold Gates, and I am a middle school student. It has always been my dream to attend your academy. I have the highest grades in my class, and I am a very hard worker. I am involved in six clubs at my school. I have included an essay and recommendation with this. I'm looking forward to hearing from your school. Thank you.

남 저의 이름은 Harold Gates이고, 중학생 입니다. 귀하의 아카데미에 입학하는 것이 언제나 저의 꿈이었습니다. 저는 반에서 점수가 가장 높으며, 굉장히 성실한 학생입니다. 저는 저희 학교에서 여섯 개의 동아리에 소속되어 있습니다. 논문과 추천서를 함께 동봉하였습니다. 저는 귀하의 학교에서 소식을 들을 수 있기를 고대합니다. 감사합니다.

Vocabulary	attend ～에 다니다 be involved in ～에 가담하다 include 포함하다 recommendation 추천서

6

M Hey, Ellen. Do you think Tara likes to go dancing?

W I don't know. Why do you ask?

M Well, I've decided to ask her out on a date, but I'm not sure where to take her. I mean,

남 있지, Ellen. Tara가 춤추는 것을 좋아할 것 같니?

여 모르겠어. 왜 물어보는 거야?

남 나 그녀에게 데이트 신청을 하기로 마음 먹었거든, 근데 난 그녀를 어디로 데려가야 할지 모르겠어. 내 말은,

I'd like to go out dancing somewhere. But she might like a movie better. I don't like going to movies, though.

W See if she says "yes," first.

M Right. I have to ask her out first.

나는 춤을 추러 가거나 하고 싶어. 그런데 그녀는 영화를 더 좋아할 수도 있잖아. 나는 영화 보러 가고 싶지 않거든.

여 그녀가 먼저 "예스"라고 하는지 봐야지.

남 맞아. 그녀에게 데이트 신청부터 먼저 해야겠지.

M Hey, Alicia, did you hear about that new comedy with Brad Pitt?

W Yeah. I want to see it. But I'm not sure when it's coming out. Do you know when that is?

M I think it's opening this Saturday. Would you like to go see it with me?

W Well, sure. I'd really like that, Dale.

M Great. I'll pick you up at 6 o'clock, then.

남 이봐, Alicia, Brad Pitt가 출연하는 새로운 코미디(영화)에 대해 들었니?

여 응. 나 그거 보고 싶어. 하지만 언제 개봉하는지 모르겠어. 너는 언제인지 아니?

남 내 생각에는 다음주 토요일에 개봉하는 것 같아. 나랑 같이 보러 갈래?

여 음. 물론이지. 정말 그러고 싶어, Dale.

남 좋아. 그럼 6시에 데리러 갈게.

M I can't wait for that Electric Fire Band show Friday night. Are you going?

W That depends. How much are tickets?

M They're just $5. And the band is going to play four new songs!

W Wow. That might be kind of cool. Where's the show?

M It's at the West End Cafe. The show starts at 8:30.

W Yeah, that sounds pretty fun. I'm looking forward to it.

남 난 금요일 밤의 Electric Fire 밴드의 쇼가 너무 기대 돼. 너도 가니?

여 봐서. 표가 얼마니?

남 5달러 밖에 안 해. 그리고 그들은 새로운 네 곡을 연주할 거야!

여 와우. 정말 멋지겠구나. 쇼가 어디에서 열려?

남 West End Cafe에서 해. 쇼는 8시 30분에 시작 해.

여 응. 꽤 재미있을 것 같아. 나도 이제 기대가 되는걸.

UNIT IV WHAT'S YOUR FAVORITE COLOR?

Check Up

p.25

01 a → c → b   **02** 1. b   2. a

03 A What is your favorite type of book?

B Hmm. My favorite type is fiction. I'm interested in fictional characters. What about you?

A I enjoy reading mystery novels.

Check Up Scripts

01

M So, what would you like to do on your trip to the city today, Sara?

W Well, I'd like to go to the museum. They have a cool dinosaur exhibit now. After that, I want to do some shopping.

M Didn't you want to visit your aunt, too?

W Yeah. I haven't seen her in a while. I can do that after shopping.

남 자. 오늘 시내 여행에서 무엇을 하고 싶니. Sarah?

여 음. 나는 박물관에 가고 싶어. 오늘 그곳에서 멋진 공룡 전시회가 열려. 그 다음에 나는 쇼핑을 좀 하고 싶어.

남 너희 이모를 방문하고 싶다고도 하지 않았니?

여 응. 난 한동안 그녀를 만나지 못했어. 쇼핑 후에 만나러 가면 돼.

> **Vocabulary**   museum 박물관   dinosaur 공룡   exhibit 전시회

02

M It's nice to meet you Cheryl. Are you ready to go out?

W Sure. I'll be ready in a minute. So, have you seen this movie before?

M Yeah. It's a nice romantic comedy. Do you like those kinds of movies?

W They're my favorite. What's your favorite kind of movie?

M I'd have to say horror movies.

남 만나서 반가워. Cheryl. 외출 준비 됐니?

여 물론이지. 이제 곧 준비가 끝나. 너는 이 영화를 전에 본 적이 있니?

남 응. 멋진 로맨틱 코미디야. 너는 그런 종류의 영화를 좋아하니?

여 내가 가장 좋아하는 거야. 네가 가장 좋아하는 영화는 무엇이니?

남 공포영화라고 할 수 있어.

> **Vocabulary**   romantic comedy 로맨틱 코미디   favorite 가장 좋아하는   horror movie 공포영화

03

A What is your favorite type of book?

B Hmm. My favorite type is fiction. I'm interested in fictional characters. What about you?

A I enjoy reading mystery novels.

A 네가 가장 좋아하는 책의 종류는 무엇이니?

B 흠. 내가 가장 좋아하는 종류는 소설이야. 나는 허구적인 인물들에 관심이 있거든. 너는?

A 나는 추리소설을 좋아해.

> **Vocabulary**   be interested in ~에 관심이 있는   fiction 허구의   character 인물   mystery novel 추리소설

1

W I heard that you sold a lot of your personal belongings.	**여** 난 네가 많은 개인 소지품을 팔았다고 들었어.
M Yeah. I sold a lot of my old books and movies. I made about $200.	**남** 응. 나의 오래된 책들과 영화를 많이 팔았지. 200달러 정도를 벌었어.
W Cool. What do you want to do with it?	**여** 좋구나. 너는 그 돈으로 무엇을 하고 싶니?
M Well, my cell phone is kind of old. I'd like to buy one of those new smart phones.	**남** 음, 내 휴대폰이 꽤 오래 되었거든. 새 스마트 폰들 중 하나로 사고 싶어.
W Yeah. You could get a really nice one with all that money.	**여** 그래. 그 돈이라면 굉장히 멋진 전화기를 살 수 있을 거야.
M I sure hope so.	**남** 나도 그랬으면 좋겠어.

> **Vocabulary**   personal 개인적인   belonging 소지품

2

W What's your favorite food, Jack?	**여** 네가 가장 좋아하는 음식이 뭐야, Jack?
M Hmm. I love gumbo.	**남** 흠. 나는 검보를 좋아해.
W What's gumbo?	**여** 검보가 뭐야?
M It's a spicy stew made with shrimp, sausage, rice, and a lot of other stuff. But I can't eat it much anymore.	**남** 새우와 소시지, 밥, 그리고 여러 다른 재료들이 들어가는 매운 스튜야. 하지만 난 더 이상 그것을 먹지 못해.
W Why not?	**여** 왜 못 먹어?
M Well, I had an operation on my stomach recently. My doctor says I have to give up spicy food for a while.	**남** 음. 내가 최근에 위 수술을 받았거든. 의사 선생님이 당분간 매운 음식은 먹지 말래.
W Oh, I'm sorry.	**여** 오, 유감이구나.

> **Vocabulary**   spicy 매운   shrimp 새우   operation 수술   stomach 위   give up 포기하다   recipe 요리법

3

W My favorite TV show is Cooking Contest. I want to be a cook, and this show teaches how to cook some amazing dishes. I always want to follow the steps, but I don't have all the necessary kitchen tools. My birthday is around the corner, though. My parents said they will buy me whatever I want for my birthday. So I'd like to ask for cooking tools for my birthday.	**여** 제가 가장 좋아하는 TV 쇼는 요리대회예요. 저는 요리사가 되고 싶은데, 이 쇼에서는 여러 멋진 음식들을 요리하는 방법을 알려줘요. 저는 매번 그 요리법을 따라 하고 싶지만, 저에게는 필요한 모든 요리도구들이 없어요. 하지만 제 생일이 곧 다가와요. 저의 부모님이 생일선물로 제가 가지고 싶은 것은 무엇이든 사주시겠다고 했어요. 그래서 저는 제 생일선물로 요리도구들을 사달라고 하고 싶어요.

4

W Excuse me, I'd like to sign up for a class.

M No problem. What kind of class would you like to join?

W Yoga, please.

M Is this your first time trying yoga?

W I'd have to say so. I've only attended two times before.

M Then you're in beginner's level.

W What's the schedule for that?

M Classes are on Monday from 5:15 p.m. to 6: 30 p.m.

W That's fine. I'll sign up for it.

여 실례합니다만, 저는 수업 등록을 하고 싶어요.

남 문제 없습니다. 어떤 수업을 등록하고 싶으세요?

여 요가요.

남 요가를 처음 해보시는 건가요?

여 그렇다고 해야 할 것 같아요. 전에 딱 두 번 수업에 참석 했었거든요.

남 그러시다면 초급반에 들어가셔야 해요.

여 초급반은 수업시간이 어떻게 되죠?

남 수업은 월요일 오후 5시 15분부터 6시 30분까지 입니 다.

여 괜찮네요. 등록할게요.

5

W Hey, Jack. What's your favorite sport?

M My favorite sport is hockey.

W Oh, I didn't know you liked hockey.

M Yeah. In fact, I wanted to be a hockey player when I was a kid. Are you interested in hockey, too?

W No, I enjoy baseball. There is actually a game tonight. You can come with us if you want.

M Sure, I'd love to.

여 이봐, Jack. 네가 가장 좋아하는 운동이 뭐야?

남 내가 가장 좋아하는 운동은 하키야.

여 오, 난 네가 하키를 좋아하는지 몰랐어.

남 응. 사실, 어렸을 때 나는 하키 선수가 되고 싶었어. 너도 하키에 관심이 있니?

여 아니, 나는 야구를 좋아해. 사실 오늘 밤에도 게임이 있어. 원한다면 너도 함께 가도 좋아.

남 물론이지, 나도 가고 싶어.

6

M Well, Cindy. I'm going to a new school next year.

W Really? Well, we're going to miss you here.

M Oh, I'm still living here. I would like to see you guys from time to time. But I also look forward to making new friends, too.

W Yeah. I suppose that will be nice.

M Yeah. It's going to be great!

남 음, Cindy. 나는 내년에 새로운 학교로 갈거야.

여 정말? 음, 우리는 여기서 너를 그리워 할 거야.

남 오, 난 여기서 계속 살 거야. 난 이따금씩 너희들을 봤으면 좋겠어. 하지만 나는 새로운 친구들을 사귀는 것도 기대가 돼.

여 맞아. 내 생각에도 좋을 것 같아.

남 응. 정말 재미있을 거야!

7

W	Well, Timmy, it's almost time to leave. What else <u>would</u> <u>you</u> <u>like</u> to see at the amusement park?	여	음, Timmy. 이제 곧 떠날 시간이란다. 놀이동산에서 무엇을 더 보고 싶니?
M	Well, I'd like <u>to</u> <u>go</u> <u>on</u> that roller coaster again.	남	음, 저는 롤러 코스터를 한번 더 타고 싶어요.
W	That's fine.	여	알겠다.
M	Can we also <u>stop</u> <u>by</u> the gift shop? And can we <u>go</u> <u>through</u> the haunted house?	남	선물가게에도 가도 될까요? 그리고 유령의 집에도 갈 수 있을까요?
W	Timmy, we have to leave soon. We've already been here for 6 hours!	여	Timmy, 우리는 곧 떠나야 한단다. 우리는 이미 6시간이나 이곳에 있었어.
M	Aww. <u>I</u> <u>didn't</u> <u>notice</u>. I was having such a good time.	남	아. 몰랐어요. 저는 너무 즐거운 시간을 보내고 있었어요.

8

| W | Okay, everyone. Let's <u>take</u> <u>a</u> <u>look</u> at our schedule for next week. Monday we're selecting topics for our projects. <u>I'd</u> <u>like</u> <u>everyone</u> to think carefully about those. Those are due next month. Also, you know you have a biology test on Wednesday. We'll have <u>a</u> <u>special</u> <u>review</u> for that on Tuesday. Thursday we will go <u>to</u> <u>the</u> <u>library</u> <u>to</u> research for our project. And of course, there is <u>no</u> <u>school</u> on Friday. | 여 | 좋아요, 여러분. 다음 주 일정을 보세요. 월요일에 우리는 프로젝트를 위한 주제를 선정할 것입니다. 저는 여러분이 주제에 대해 신중하게 생각을 하셨으면 좋겠군요. 주제는 다음달까지 정하시면 됩니다. 또한, 수요일에 생물 시험이 있다는 것을 알 거에요. 우리는 그것을 위해 화요일에 특별히 복습하는 시간을 가질 거에요. 목요일에는 우리는 우리의 프로젝트를 위한 리서치를 하기 위해 도서관에 갈 거에요. 금요일에는 물론 수업이 없습니다. |

UNIT V OH, I APOLOGIZE!

p.31

🔅 Check Up

01 a   **02** 1. T 2. T

03 A Did you pick up the groceries I asked you to get?

B Oh, I'm sorry, I forgot. I apologize for that.

A Never mind.

B Well, should I go buy something now?

A That's okay. I'll try to cook something up.

Check Up Scripts

01

M Hey, Jill, did you ever mail that letter?

W Oh, I'm sorry. I forgot to drop it in the mailbox. And I think they already picked up the mail.

M Ah, that's all right. I'm about to go out, anyway. I can just drop it off at the post office. Do you still have it?

W Sure. It's right here.

남 이봐, Jill, 그 편지 이미 부쳤니?

여 오, 미안해. 우체통에 넣는다는 걸 깜박했어. 내 생각에 우체부들이 벌써 편지를 수거해 갔을 것 같은데.

남 아, 괜찮아. 나 외출하려는 참이거든. 내가 우체국에서 부치면 돼. 편지 가지고 있니?

여 그럼. 여기 있어.

Vocabulary	forget 깜먹다, 잊어버리다 drop (아래로) 떨어뜨리다 pick up 수거하다 be about to 막 ~하려고 하다 drop off 맡기다

02

W Do you need help with something, sir?

M Yes. Do you sell any DVD recorders at this store?

W I'm sorry, sir. We don't carry any DVD recorders in our electronics section.

M No problem. I wasn't going to buy one. I was just curious. Thanks, anyway.

여 도와드릴까요, 손님?

남 네. 이 가게에서 DVD 녹화기도 판매하시나요?

여 죄송합니다, 손님. 저희 전자제품 코너에서는 DVD 리코더를 취급하지 않습니다.

남 괜찮습니다. 사려고 했던 것은 아니었습니다. 그저 궁금했을 뿐이에요. 아무튼 감사합니다.

Vocabulary	carry 취급하다 electronics 전자기기 section 코너 curious 궁금한

03

A Did you pick up the groceries I asked you to get?

B Oh, I'm sorry, I forgot. I apologize for that.

A Never mind.

B Well, should I go buy something now?

A That's okay. I'll try to cook something up.

A 내가 부탁한 식료품 사왔니?

B 오, 미안해. 잊어버렸어. 정말 미안해.

A 괜찮아.

B 음, 지금 가서 뭐라도 사올까?

A 아니야. 내가 뭐라도 만들어 볼게.

Vocabulary	pick up 사다 grocery 식료품점 apologize 사과하다, 용서를 구하다 cook up 요리하다

1

M Hey. I'm here to return this book.	남 저기요. 이 책 반납하려고요.
W Okay, sir. Oh, this book is three days overdue. There's a twenty cent fine on it.	여 알겠습니다. 손님. 오, 이 책은 3일 연체 되었네요. 20센트의 벌금이 있습니다.
M What? That's not fair! I couldn't return it earlier because I was out of town!	남 뭐라고요? 너무해요! 더 일찍 반납을 못한 이유는 제가 이 도시에 없었기 때문이에요!
W There's no fine for just one day. After that, though, you need to pay ten cents a day. I'm sorry.	여 하루 정도는 연체료가 부과되지 않아요. 하지만 그 후에는, 하루당 10센트의 벌금을 내셔야 해요. 죄송합니다.
M Never mind. I'll just pay the fine.	남 놔두세요. 그냥 연체료를 낼게요.

> **Vocabulary** return 반납하다, 돌려주다   overdue (반납 등의) 기한이 지난   fine 벌금, 과태료   out of town 지방의, 출장중인

2

W Terry, I didn't receive your chemistry paper yesterday.	여 Terry, 난 어제 네 화학 과제를 못 받았단다.
M I'm sorry, Ms. Hines. I wasn't able to finish it in time because of my operation last week.	남 죄송해요, Hines선생님. 지난 주에 수술을 받아서 제 시간 내에 과제를 끝내지 못했어요.
W That's OK. But you should have let me know sooner. I'll give you until Friday to finish it.	여 괜찮단다. 하지만 더 일찍 나에게 말을 했어야 해. 그것을 끝낼 수 있도록 금요일까지 시간을 주도록 하마.
M Thanks. That should be enough time.	남 고맙습니다. 충분한 시간이에요.

> **Vocabulary** receive 받다   chemistry 화학   paper 과제, 리포트   operation 수술   enough 충분한

3

M Excuse me, miss? This steak is too dark for me.	남 저기요, 종업원 아가씨. 이 스테이크는 너무 익혀졌어요.
W I don't understand. Didn't you want it cooked well done?	여 무슨 말씀이세요. 바싹 익혀 달라고 하지 않으셨어요?
M Actually, no. I only asked for medium rare. I like my steak to be a little red.	남 아닌데요. 저는 약간 덜 익혀 달라고 말씀 드렸어요. 저는 스테이크가 덜 익은 것이 좋거든요.
W Oh, that's right. I apologize, sir. I'll go back and get them to cook you a new steak right away.	여 오, 맞아요. 죄송합니다. 손님. 제가 바로 가서 새로운 스테이크로 구워달라고 말씀 드리겠습니다.

> **Vocabulary** well done (고기가) 완전히 익힌   medium rare (고기가) 약간 덜 익힌   right away 당장   complain 불평하다

4

M	Is everything OK. ma'am?	**남**	별 문제 없으신가요, 부인?
W	Actually, my suitcase is up there, but I am not able to reach it.	**여**	실은, 제 여행가방이 저 위에 있는데, 제 손이 닿지가 않네요.
M	Oh, I'm sorry. Here, let me help you with that.	**남**	오, 죄송합니다. 제가 도와 드리겠습니다.
W	Thanks. Also, when will dinner be served on this flight?	**여**	고맙습니다. 그리고, 이 비행기에서는 식사가 언제 제공되나요?
M	Not for a few hours. But we can get you a little snack and some water in a minute, if you want.	**남**	몇 시간 후에 제공됩니다. 하지만 원하신다면 간단한 간식과 식수를 가져다 드릴 수 있습니다.
W	Thank you. I'd appreciate that.	**여**	고맙습니다. 그래 주시면 감사하죠.

Vocabulary	suitcase 여행가방　reach (손이) 닿다　serve 제공하다　flight 비행, 비행기　appreciate 고마워하다

5

W	Um, Gerald? Please forgive me. I accidentally lost that jacket you lent me. I'm sorry.	**여**	음, Gerald? 용서해줘. 실수로 네가 빌려줬던 재킷을 잃어버렸어. 미안해.
M	Forget it. It was old and worn out anyway.	**남**	괜찮아. 어차피 오래되고 낡은 옷이었는걸.
W	Yeah, but I still feel bad about it. Listen, I can pay for a new one, if you like.	**여**	응, 하지만 내 마음이 안 좋아서. 그래서 네가 원한다면 새로운 재킷을 사줄게.
M	Thanks, but that might not be necessary. I think my uncle will give me one of his.	**남**	고맙지만, 필요 없을 것 같아. 우리 삼촌이 나에게 그의 재킷 하나를 줄 것 같거든.

Vocabulary	accidentally 실수로, 우연히　jacket 재킷　worn out 낡은　anyway 어차피　pay for ～의 돈을 지불하다

6

①	**M**	I'm sorry to lose your cell phone. It was my fault.	①	**남**	네 휴대폰을 잃어버렸는데 미안해. 내 실수였어.
	W	What? How could you do that?		**여**	뭐라고? 너 어떻게 그럴 수가 있어?
②	**M**	Hey, did you hear that Mike won the prize this time?	②	**남**	야, Mike가 이번에 우승을 했다는 거 들었어?
	W	That's not fair! I also did my best!		**여**	너무해! 나도 최선을 다했는데!
③	**M**	I apologize that I didn't call you last night.	③	**남**	어제 밤에 전화 못해서 미안해요.
	W	It doesn't matter. I went to sleep early.		**여**	괜찮아요. 제가 어제 일찍 잤거든요.
④	**M**	I'm sorry, Jessica. I broke your MP3 player.	④	**남**	미안해, Jessica. 내가 너의 MP3 플레이어를 고장 냈어.
	W	Never mind. I was going to buy a new one.		**여**	신경 쓰지마. 새 것으로 사려고 했었거든.

⑤ **M** Mom, please forgive me for my test results.

   W That's OK. You just need to study harder.

⑤ **남** 엄마, 제 시험 성적을 용서해주세요.

   여 괜찮단다. 너는 단지 더 열심히 공부할 필요가 있어.

Vocabulary	cell phone 휴대폰　　fault 실수　　win the prize 우승하다　　matter 문제되다, 중요하다　　forgive 용서하다 result 결과

7

M Hey, Janet. Did you want to talk to me?

W Yes! Didn't you know that yesterday was my birthday? Why didn't you come to my party, Mark? I was really hoping you'd show up.

M I'm sorry. I forgot all about it.

W What? How could you do that? I thought you were one of my closest friends!

M Yeah, I know. I don't know how it happened.

W This is unbelievable! I'm so disappointed in you!

남 이봐, Janet. 나와 얘기하길 원했니?

여 응! 너 어제가 내 생일이었다는 거 몰랐니? 어제 왜 내 생일파티에 오지 않은 거야, Mark? 난 네가 오기를 정말 바랬단 말이야.

남 미안해. 나 깜박했어.

여 뭐라고? 어떻게 그럴 수가 있니? 난 네가 나의 가장 친한 친구들 중 한 명이라고 생각했는데.

남 응, 알아. 나도 어떻게 그런 일이 일어났는지 모르겠어.

여 믿을 수가 없어! 나는 너에게 정말 실망했어!

Vocabulary	show up 나타나다, 모습을 보이다　　forget 잊다, 깜박하다　　happen 일어나다　　unbelievable 믿을 수 없는 disappointed 실망한

8

W Last week I tried out for my school's volleyball team. I did really well. In fact, I was better than anyone else there. I was going to be on the team, but something happened. I fell off my bike yesterday and badly broke my arm. Now I can't play this year at all. It's not fair! I was looking forward to this for a long time.

여 지난 주에, 나는 학교 배구 팀에 지원을 했습니다. 나는 굉장히 잘 했습니다. 사실, 그곳에 있던 그 누구보다 내가 제일 잘 했습니다. 나는 팀에 합류할 수 있었는데, 일이 생겼습니다. 나는 어제 자전거에서 떨어져 팔을 심하게 다쳤습니다. 이제 나는 올해에는 배구를 할 수가 없습니다. 이건 너무 해요! 나는 오랫동안 이것을 바래 왔었는데 말입니다.

Vocabulary	try out for ~에 지원하다　　fall off ~에서 떨어지다　　badly 심하게

UNIT VI MAY I TAKE YOUR ORDER?

Check Up

p.37

01 a **02** 1. grilled steak   2. restaurant

03 A Good morning, sir. Can I take your order?

B Yes, I'd like to have pancakes with some coffee, please.

A Of course, sir. For here or to go?

B For here, please.

Check Up Scripts

01

M Hello, ma'am. May I take your order, please?

W Sure. I think I will just have a small order of fries.

M Alright. Would you be interested in trying one of our milkshakes, too?

W Hmm. Actually, I would. Can I get a vanilla milkshake with those fries, please?

남 안녕하세요. 부인. 주문하시겠어요?

여 네. 전 그냥 감자튀김만 주문하려고요.

남 알겠습니다. 저희 밀크셰이크도 한번 드셔 보시지 않으시겠어요?

여 흠. 먹어볼게요. 감자튀김이랑 같이 바닐라 밀크셰이크 한 잔 주시겠어요?

Vocabulary	order 주문 be interested in ~에 흥미가 있는 actually 사실

02

W Hello, sir. Are you ready to order?

M Not yet. What's today's special?

W We have a grilled steak with chicken salad.

M OK. I'll have it.

W Sure, will there be anything else?

M No, that's all.

여 안녕하세요. 손님. 주문하시겠어요?

남 아직이요. 오늘의 요리가 무엇이죠?

여 치킨 샐러드를 곁들인 구운 스테이크입니다.

남 좋아요. 그걸로 할게요.

여 물론이죠, 더 필요한 건 없으십니까?

남 없어요. 그게 다에요.

Vocabulary	grilled 구운

03

A Good morning, sir. Can I take your order?

B Yes, I'd like to have pancakes with some coffee, please.

A Of course, sir. For here or to go?

B For here, please.

A 좋은 아침입니다. 손님. 주문하시겠어요?

B 네, 저는 팬 케이크와 커피 한잔 부탁해요.

A 물론입니다. 손님. 여기서 드시고 가시겠습니까 아니면 포장하시겠습니까?

B 여기서 먹고 갈게요.

Actual Test
1 ①   2 ③   3 ③   4 ①   5 ④   6 ①   7 ③   8 ① | p.38

1

[Telephone rings.]

W Golden Dragon Chinese Restaurant. This is Christine speaking. May I take your order?

M Yes. I'd like to have two orders of orange chicken, mixed vegetables, and fried rice.

W All right, sir. It should be ready in 20 minutes.

M Great. I'd like to pick it up, but I need directions to your restaurant, please.

W Certainly, sir. Go north on Highway 18. Then turn left on Highway 16. Take a right on Dogwood Road. We're located in that shopping center.

M Thank you.

Vocabulary	Chinese 중국의 vegetable 야채 fried 볶은, 튀긴 direction (위치, 이동의) 방향 highway 고속도로 be located in ~에 위치해 있다

[전화벨 소리]

여 Golden Dragon 중식당 입니다. 저는 Christine입니다. 주문하시겠어요?

남 네. 오렌지 치킨, 모듬 야채, 그리고 볶음밥으로 2개 주세요.

여 알겠습니다. 손님. 20분 후에 준비될 겁니다.

남 좋군요. 가지러 가려고 하는데요, 식당으로 가는 길 좀 알려주세요.

여 물론이죠. 18번 고속도로 북쪽으로 오세요. 16번 고속도로에서 좌회전 하시고요. Dogwood도로에서 우회전 하세요. 저희는 그 쇼핑센터 내에 위치해 있습니다.

남 고맙습니다.

2

M Can I take your order, ma'am?

W Uh, not yet. I'm still waiting for my friend to arrive. But could I possibly get some bread for an appetizer?

M Of course, ma'am. Do you need another menu, too?

W No, that won't be necessary. She can just use mine. Thanks anyway.

Vocabulary	wait for ~을 기다리다 arrive 도착하다 possibly (최대한) 가능한대로 appetizer 에피타이저, 전채요리 necessary 필요한

남 주문하시겠습니까, 부인?

여 어, 아직이요. 저는 아직 제 친구가 도착하길 기다리고 있어요. 하지만 에피타이저로 빵을 좀 가져다 주실 수 있을까요?

남 물론이지요. 부인. 다른 메뉴판이 하나 더 필요하신가요?

여 아니요, 필요 없을 것 같아요. 그녀가 제 것을 같이 보면 되요. 어쨌든 고맙습니다.

3

M May I take your order?

W Yes. I'd like to have this grilled salmon with rice, please.

M Excellent choice. Now, you get two sides with this.

W Let's see. I'll have a salad for one of the sides. And what kind of soups do you have today?

M We have black bean soup and tomato soup.

W Okay. I'll have the tomato soup, then.

남 주문하시겠습니까?

여 네. 저는 밥을 곁들인 구운 연어로 할게요.

남 탁월한 선택이십니다. 이제, 두 가지의 곁들임 요리를 선택하시면 됩니다.

여 어디 보자. 하나는 샐러드로 주시고요. 오늘은 어떤 종류의 수프가 있나요?

남 검은 콩과 토마토 수프가 준비되어 있습니다.

여 좋아요. 저는 토마토 수프로 주세요, 그럼.

4

[The answering machine beeps.]

M Hello. My name is Jason Williams, and I'd like to place an order. This is for take-out. I also have a coupon for five dollars off. I'd like two large pizzas, please. I want to have vegetables only on one of them. The other should be shrimp gold, please.

[자동응답기 소리]

남 여보세요. 제 이름은 Jason Williams이고요, 주문을 하고 싶어요. 포장해주세요. 저에게는 5달러짜리 할인 쿠폰도 있습니다. 라지 피자로 두 개 주문합니다. 한 쪽에는 야채만 토핑 해주세요. 또 다른 하나는 쉬림프 골드로 부탁합니다.

5

① **M** Can I take your order, ma'am?

   W I'll have a coffee, please.

② **W** Can I have a burrito and taco combo, please?

   M Yes, ma'am. For here or to go?

③ **W** Are you ready to order?

   M No, I'd like a few more minutes to decide.

④ **W** I'd like to have some shrimp pasta, please.

   M Can I take your order?

⑤ **M** How would you like your steak, ma'am?

   W Well done, please.

① **남** 주문하시겠어요, 부인?

   여 커피 한 잔 주세요.

② **여** 부리토하고 타코 콤보로 주시겠어요?

   남 네. 손님. 여기서 드시고 가시겠습니까 아니면 포장해드릴까요?

③ **여** 주문하실 준비가 되었나요?

   남 아니요. 결정하려면 시간이 좀 더 필요해요.

④ **여** 새우 파스타로 주세요.

   남 주문하시겠어요?

⑤ **남** 스테이크 굽기는 어떻게 해드릴까요, 손님?

   여 바싹 익혀주세요.

6

W Hi, welcome to Frankie's. Are you ready to order?

M Can you recommend one?

W How about the "volcano burger"? It's very hot but most people love it.

M Well, I think my stomach can't handle spicy food.

W What about beef steak then? It comes with a baked potato.

M It sounds good. I'll have it.

여 어서 오세요, Frankie's에 오신 것을 환영합니다. 주문하시겠어요?

남 하나 추천해 주시겠어요?

여 볼케이노 버거 어떠세요? 굉장히 맵지만. 대부분의 사람들이 좋아하지요.

남 음. 제 위가 매운 음식은 못 견딜 것 같아요.

여 그럼 소고기 스테이크는 어떠세요? 구운 감자와 함께 나옵니다.

남 맛있을 것 같네요. 그걸로 할게요.

M May I take your order, ma'am?

W Yes. I'd like to have a slice of pie and coffee, please.

M What kind of pie would you like?

W Hmm. I think I'll have the peach pie.

M All right. And what size coffee?

W Just a medium. And can I have some whipped cream on the pie, too?

M You got it.

남	주문하시겠습니까, 부인?

남 주문하시겠습니까, 부인?

여 네. 파이 한 조각과 커피 한잔 부탁 드려요.

남 어떤 종류의 파이로 드릴까요?

여 흠. 저는 복숭아 파이로 할게요.

남 알겠습니다. 커피는 어떤 사이즈로 드릴까요?

여 중간 크기로 주세요. 그리고 파이 위에 휩 크림도 올려 주시겠어요?

남 알겠습니다.

Vocabulary	a slice of 한 조각의 peach 복숭아 medium 중간 whipped cream 휩 크림

M Excuse me. Do you serve any vegetarian dishes here?

W Yes, sir. We have a special vegetarian section on our menu.

M Great. How is the Thai vegetable stir fry?

W It's excellent, sir.

M Does it have any peanuts in it? I'm allergic to peanuts.

W Oh, yes. The dish has peanuts in it.

M Ah, let me see what other vegetarian dishes you have then.

남 저기요. 이곳에 채식주의자들을 위한 요리가 있나요?

여 예. 있습니다. 저희 메뉴에는 특별한 채식주의자용 섹션이 있습니다.

남 좋네요. 태국식 야채볶음은 어떤가요?

여 정말 맛있습니다. 손님.

남 안에 땅콩이 들어가나요? 제가 땅콩 알레르기가 있어서요.

여 그렇습니다. 이 음식에는 땅콩이 사용됩니다.

남 아. 그럼 다른 채식주의 음식은 무엇이 있는지 좀 볼게요.

Vocabulary	vegetarian 채식주의자 peanut 땅콩 allergic 알레르기가 있는

UNIT VII DO I HAVE TO STUDY?

01 1. a 2. c 3. b **02** she was meeting with her teacher.

03 A Hey, <u>when should I</u> submit the report?

  B <u>You have to submit</u> it by this Friday.

  A Then I think <u>I should</u> start on Thursday.

  B What? <u>You have to start</u> today. You cannot finish it in one day.

Check Up Scripts

01

W Hey, Jerry, I'm having dinner with some friends on Monday. Care to join us?

M Sorry, I can't. I have an appointment that night. By the way, are you going do the report for science class on Friday?

W Yes, I am. I was going to do it on Thursday, but I had to switch days. I'm going to visit my grandmother at hospital on Thursday.

M Oh. I hope she's OK.

여 이봐, Jerry. 나 월요일에 몇몇 친구들이랑 저녁식사를 같이 할거야. 너도 올래?

남 미안하지만, 난 못 가. 나 그날 약속이 있거든. 그건 그렇고, 너 금요일 날 과학수업 레포트 할 거니?

여 응. 그러려구. 난 목요일에 하려고 했는데 요일을 바꿔야 했어. 목요일에는 병원에 입원 중이신 할머니 병문안을 가거든.

남 오. 할머님이 괜찮으셨으면 좋겠다.

Vocabulary	by the way 그건 그렇고 tutor 가정교사 usually 주로, 대개 switch 바꾸다 hospital 병원

02

W Thanks for picking me up, dad. I'm sorry I missed the school bus again.

M That's alright, Hillary. But you must not miss the bus anymore. I can't pick you up every day.

W I know. But I had to talk to Ms. Reynolds about my homework.

M I understand. And it wasn't a problem today.

여 저를 데리러 와주셔서 감사해요, 아빠. 제가 또 스쿨버스를 놓쳐서 죄송해요.

남 괜찮다, Hillary. 하지만 더 이상은 버스를 놓치면 안 된다. 내가 매일 너를 데리러 올 수는 없단다.

여 알아요. 하지만 저는 Reynolds 선생님과 숙제에 관해 이야기를 했어야 했어요.

남 이해한다. 오늘은 괜찮단다.

Vocabulary	pick somebody up ～를 차에 태우러 가다 miss 놓치다

03

A Hey, when should I submit the report?

B You have to submit it by this Friday.

A Then I think I should start on Thursday.

B What? You have to start today. You cannot finish it in one day.

A 이봐, 우리 리포트 언제 제출해야 해?

B 이번 주 금요일까지 제출하면 돼.

A 그럼 목요일에 시작하면 되겠네.

B 뭐라고? 너 오늘 시작해야 해. 하루 만에 끝낼 수 없어.

Vocabulary	submit 제출하다

M Okay, we've only got five minutes to get to your school. I'll have to drive really fast.

W Whoa! What are you doing? Didn't you see that sign back there? You are supposed to stop there.

M Oh, you're right! I didn't stop at that sign.

W We're lucky, Dad. We didn't hit another car or get caught by the police.

남 좋아. 네 학교까지 5분 안에 도착해야 해. 나는 운전을 굉장히 빨리 해야 해.

여 우왜! 지금 뭐 하시는 거에요? 뒤에 있는 저 표지만 못 보셨어요? 아빠는 저기에서 정지 했어야 해요.

남 오, 네 말이 맞아! 나는 표지판에서 정지하지 않았구나.

여 운이 좋은 거에요, 아빠. 다른 차를 들이받지도, 경찰에 잡히지도 않았잖아요.

> Vocabulary   be supposed to ~해야만 한다   sign 표지판   get caught 잡히다

M Linda, I heard that your sister was offered a new job.

W Yeah, but she's not sure about it. I don't think she will take this new job.

M I don't understand. Doesn't it pay a lot more money?

W Yes, but she said she is not ready for it.

M But she has children. This new job could help support her family. I think she should take it.

W Yeah, you've got a good point.

남 Linda, 너희 언니가 새로운 직장을 소개 받았다고 들었어.

여 응. 그런데 그녀는 잘 모르겠나 봐. 그녀는 그 새로운 직장으로 가지 않을 것 같아.

남 이해가 안돼. 그곳이 훨씬 더 많은 돈을 주지 않니?

여 응. 하지만 그녀는 준비가 되지 않았대.

남 하지만 그녀에게는 자식들이 있잖아. 새로운 직장은 그녀의 가족들을 부양하는데 도움이 될 거야. 난 그녀가 그 제의를 받아들여야 한다고 생각해.

여 그래, 네 말에 일리가 있어.

> Vocabulary   offer 제공하다   be ready for ~를 위한 준비가 되다   support 부양하다, 지원하다

M Hi. I need a room for the night.

W Yes, sir. That will be $80, please.

M Okay. Will you take this credit card?

W Of course, sir. You can watch TV in the lobby, but the Internet is not connected now.

M That's fine. When should I be out?

W You have to check out by 12:00 p.m., sir.

남 안녕하세요. 하룻밤 묵을 방이 필요해요.

여 알겠습니다, 손님. 80달러 입니다.

남 네. 신용카드도 받으시나요?

여 물론입니다, 손님. 로비에 있는 TV를 시청하실 수 있지만, 인터넷은 현재 연결되어 있지 않습니다.

남 괜찮습니다. 언제 방을 비워줘야 하나요?

여 오후 12시까지 체크아웃 하시면 됩니다, 손님.

> Vocabulary   credit card 신용카드   Internet 인터넷   connect 연결하다   check out 체크아웃 하다

4

M These very large animals <u>can be found</u> in the woods, mountains, and other places <u>in nature</u>. They live all over the world. <u>They are covered</u> in thick fur, and they can walk <u>on two legs</u> or four legs. Some of them sleep during <u>the whole winter</u>. They eat all kinds of things, like fish, berries, honey, and even garbage. You should <u>be careful of</u> them because they sometimes attack people.

남 이 거대한 동물들은 숲, 산, 그리고 자연의 다른 장소들에서 발견할 수 있습니다. 그들은 세계 곳곳에 살고 있습니다. 그들은 두터운 털로 덮여 있으며, 두 개 혹은 네 개의 다리로 걸을 수 있습니다. 어떤 이들은 겨울 내내 잠을 잡니다. 그들은 생선, (딸기)열매, 꿀, 심지어 쓰레기와 같이 다양한 것들을 먹습니다. 그들은 때때로 사람을 공격하기도 하므로, 여러분은 그들을 경계해야 합니다.

Vocabulary	animal 동물 mountain 산 nature 자연 be covered in ~으로 덮여있다 fur 털 garbage 쓰레기 be careful of ~을 경계하다 attack 공격하다

5

W Good morning, everyone. <u>Before I start</u>, I'd like to ask a question. Whenever we send a fax, <u>are we supposed</u> to have an actual fax machine? <u>Not anymore</u>. Today, we're going to learn about new Internet faxing programs. You can <u>download faxes</u> very simply with this program. They also let you <u>send</u> and <u>receive</u> faxes through your email address. If you don't have enough money to buy a fax machine, if you don't know <u>how to use</u> one, this will be very useful.

여 좋은 아침이에요, 여러분. 시작하기 전에, 저는 여러분에게 질문을 하나 하고 싶군요. 우리가 팩스를 보낼 때마다, 우리는 실제의 팩스기계를 가지고 있어야 하나요? 더 이상은 아니에요. 오늘, 우리는 새로운 인터넷 팩스 프로그램에 대해 배울 것 입니다. 여러분은 이 프로그램을 이용하여 팩스를 굉장히 쉽게 다운로드를 할 수 있습니다. 또한 이메일 주소만으로 팩스를 주고 받게도 해줍니다. 팩스기계를 장만할 충분한 돈이 없으시거나, 어떻게 사용하는지 모르신다면, 이것은 굉장히 유용할 것입니다.

Vocabulary	actual 실제의 fax machine 팩스 기계 download 다운로드하다 simply 쉽게 receive 받다 useful 유용한

6

① **M** Mom, <u>how should I study</u> for the exam?
   W You have to <u>review the lessons</u> and study for it.

② **M** You're not <u>supposed to use</u> your cell phone in the library.
   W Oh, sorry. I'll take this call outside, then.

③ **W** You <u>should not watch</u> TV before doing your homework.
   M Okay. I'll start on my homework right away.

④ **W** Mr. White, am I supposed to <u>complete the report</u> by Monday?
   M Yes, I will not accept late reports.

① **남** 엄마, 시험 공부는 어떻게 해야 해요?
   여 수업을 복습하고 공부를 해야지.

② **남** 도서관에서는 휴대폰을 사용하실 수 없어요.
   여 오, 죄송해요. 그럼 이 전화를 나가서 받도록 할게요.

③ **여** 네 숙제를 하기 전에는 TV를 보면 안돼.
   남 알겠어요. 지금 당장 숙제를 할게요.

④ **여** White교수님, 제가 월요일까지 리포트를 완성해야 하나요?
   남 그래, 제출이 늦은 리포트는 받지 않을 거야.

⑤ **W** I need to speak with someone right away.

M Sorry, ma'am. You must <u>wait in line</u> like everyone else here.

⑤ **여** 저는 당장 누군가와 통화를 해야 해요.

남 죄송합니다. 부인. 하지만 다른 사람들처럼 이곳에 줄을 서야 합니다.

Vocabulary	review 복습하다 lesson 수업, 강의 library 도서관 right away 당장 complete 완성하다, 끝내다.
	accept 받아들이다. wait in line 줄을 서다

W Mike, <u>come here a minute</u>, please.

M What is it, Mom?

W <u>Did you pinch</u> your little brother?

M Well, yeah. But he <u>kept playing</u> with my toys! I told him to stop, but <u>he wouldn't</u>.

W That doesn't matter. You're a lot bigger than he is. You <u>should not hurt</u> him, ever.

M OK, Mom. I'm sorry.

여 Mike, 잠깐 이리로 좀 와볼래?

남 무슨 일인데요, 엄마?

여 네가 네 남동생을 꼬집었니?

남 음, 네. 하지만 그가 자꾸 제 장난감을 가지고 놀았어요! 제가 그에게 그만하라고 했는데, 말을 듣지 않았단 말이에요.

여 그건 상관 없어. 넌 그보다 훨씬 더 형이잖니. 넌 그를 다치게 해서는 절대 안돼.

남 알았어요. 엄마. 죄송해요.

Vocabulary	pinch 꼬집다 keep ~ing 계속해서 ~을 하다 hurt 다치게 하다

W Rudy, did you want to <u>talk to</u> me?

M Yes, Ms. Scott. Well, I think I can't <u>finish my project</u> by March 8th. It is a very big project. It will <u>take a long time</u> to finish it.

W I know. I will give you more time. <u>Let me see</u>. Today is March 4th. Well, I will allow you to submit the project <u>by next</u> Friday. But remember this. You have to finish it by then.

M Sure. Thank you.

여 Rudy, 나와 얘기를 하고 싶어했니?

남 네, Scott 선생님. 제 생각에는 제 프로젝트를 3월 8일까지 끝낼 수 없을 것 같아요. 끝내려면 오랜 시간이 걸릴 거에요.

여 그래 나도 안다. 시간을 더 주마. 어디 보자, 오늘이 3월 4일이지. 그럼, 다음주 금요일까지 제출하는 것을 허락해 주마. 하지만 이것을 기억해라. 그때까지는 끝내야 한다.

남 물론이지요. 감사합니다.

Vocabulary	take time 시간이 걸리다 finish 끝내다 remember 기억하다

UNIT VIII I DON'T THINK SO.

✦ Check Up

01 a   **02** 1. woman   2. man

03 A Did you find today's lecture interesting?

B I think it was pretty interesting. What did you think about it?

A I'm with you. I usually daydream during class. But I really enjoyed the lecture, too.

Check Up Scripts

01

M I really liked that movie.

W Yeah, I think it was good. I loved watching *The Sound of Music*. You know, we can also see the stage version in the city.

M Really? I've never seen it before. Do you want to get tickets for it this Friday?

W Sure!

남 나는 영화가 너무 재미있었어.

여 응, 나도 괜찮았던 것 같아. 「사운드 오브 뮤직」을 보는 것이 아주 재미있었어. 있잖아, 우리는 시내에서 연극판도 볼 수 있어.

남 정말? 나 그거 본 적 없는데. 이번 주 금요일 표 사지 않을래?

여 좋지!

Vocabulary	stage version 연극판

02

M Did you hear the news? They're tearing down the old playground and building a restaurant there.

W Oh, that's nice. We need more restaurants here.

M Well, I'm against it. I love playing at that playground with my friends. Where else can we hang out?

W Huh. I suppose that our opinions just differ.

남 너 소식 들었니? 낡은 놀이터를 허물고 그곳에 식당을 지을 거래.

여 오, 잘됐네. 여기에는 식당이 더 많이 필요하잖아.

남 음, 난 반대야. 나는 내 친구들과 그 놀이터에서 노는 것을 좋아해. 우리가 다른 어느 곳에서 놀 수가 있니?

여 허. 내 생각에는 우리 의견이 다른 것 뿐이라고 생각해.

Vocabulary	tear down 허물다 playground 놀이터 suppose ~이라고 생각하다 differ 다르다

03

A Did you find today's lecture interesting?

B I think it was pretty interesting. What did you think about it?

A I'm with you. I usually daydream during class. But I really enjoyed the lecture, too.

A 너는 오늘 강의가 재미있었니?

B 나는 꽤 흥미로웠던 것 같아. 너는 어떻게 생각했니?

A 나도 네 말에 동의해. 나는 수업 시간에는 대부분 공상에 잠기거든. 그런데 이번 강의는 정말 재미있었어.

Vocabulary	lecture 강의 pretty 꽤 daydream 공상하다

Actual Test

1 ⑤   2 ②   3 ⑤   4 ③   5 ①   6 ③   7 ④   8 ③

| p.50

1

W What do you think of this couch, George?

M Hmm. I think it's the wrong color. I don't want a black couch.

W Well, I agree with you. We need something lighter.

M How about this over here?

W George, that's not big enough. Two people can't sit on that.

M Ah! This is the perfect size, and it's just the right color, too.

W You're right! I love it.

M I'll see if a clerk can help us with it.

여 이 소파 어떤 것 같아, George?

남 흠. 내 생각에는 색상이 별로인 것 같아. 나는 검은색 소파는 싫어.

여 음. 나도 같은 생각이야. 우리에게는 조금 더 밝은 색상의 것이 필요해.

남 이쪽에 있는 이것은 어때?

여 George, 그건 작잖아. 두 사람이 앉을 수가 없어.

남 아! 이게 완벽한 사이즈야. 그리고 색상도 맞네.

여 네 말이 맞아! 나 그거 좋아.

남 점원에게 우리를 도와줄 수 있는지 확인해볼게.

2

M Well, I had a fun time at the beach this weekend. What did you think?

W Yeah, the weather was nice for swimming and surfing.

M What did you think about the fishing there?

W Hmm. Fishing is my favorite hobby, but I didn't enjoy it much this time.

M Me, neither. There were not many good fishing spots.

남 음. 나는 이번 주말에 해변에서 정말 즐거웠어. 너는 어땠니?

여 응. 날씨가 수영과 파도타기를 하기에 참 좋았어.

남 그곳에서의 낚시는 어땠던 것 같니?

여 흠. 낚시는 내가 가장 좋아하는 취미이지만, 나는 이번에는 그리 즐기지 못했어.

남 나도 마찬가지야. 좋은 낚시터가 많이 없었어.

3

W Our town has had a recycling program for nearly 40 years. Now our new mayor wants to stop it. He says that it costs too much money. But this recycling program greatly lowers the amount of trash in our city. We need it to save materials and keep the environment clean. That's why I don't like the idea of ending the program.

여 우리 도시는 거의 40년 동안 재활용 프로그램을 운영하고 있습니다. 현재 우리의 새로운 시장은 그 프로그램을 중단하고 싶어합니다. 그는 그것에 상당한 비용이 든다고 말을 합니다. 하지만 이 재활용 프로그램은 우리 도시의 쓰레기 양을 크게 감소시킵니다. 우리는 자재를 절약하고 환경을 청결하게 유지하기 위해 그것이 필요합니다. 그래서 나는 이 프로그램을 중단한다는 생각은 좋지 않다고 생각합니다.

4

M That was quite a baseball game! Did you find it exciting, Tammy?

W Oh, I did. The Braves and Cubs played an amazing game. I just wish it had not started so late.

M Yeah. 8:00 p.m. is a pretty late starting time for a Wednesday night.

W Still, they sold hot dogs for half price tonight. That was pretty nice.

M Yeah. I also liked the new big TV screen they had. That was pretty cool!

남 꽤 괜찮은 야구경기였어! 너도 재미있었지, Tammy?

여 응. 재밌었어. Braves와 Cubs는 정말 멋진 경기를 펼쳤어. 단지 경기가 그렇게 늦게만 하지 않았으면 좋았을걸.

남 응. 오후 8시는 수요일 밤의 시작 시간으로는 꽤 늦은 거지.

여 하지만, 오늘 밤에는 핫도그를 반값에 판매했잖아. 그건 꽤 맛있었어.

남 응. 나는 새로운 대형 TV 화면도 좋았어. 꽤 근사하더라!

| Vocabulary | quite 상당한, 꽤 | exciting 재미있는 | amazing 멋진 | pretty 꽤 | half price 반값, 절반 가격 | stadium 경기장 |

5

M I don't know about this cake. Do you think it will taste good?

W I think so. Everyone loves your cakes.

M Yeah, maybe you're right. There will be plenty of other dishes, anyway.

W Yeah. By the way, I think it's really good for us to gather once a year.

M I agree with you. It's good to spend time with all of the family members.

남 난 이 케이크가 어떨지 잘 모르겠어. 너는 이 케이크가 맛이 있을 거라고 생각하니?

여 난 그렇게 생각해. 모든 사람들이 네 케이크를 좋아하잖아.

남 그래. 네 말이 맞을지도 몰라. 어쨌든 다른 요리들도 많이 있을 테니까.

여 응. 그나저나, 나는 이렇게 일년에 한 번씩 모이는 게 참 좋은 것 같아.

남 나도 네 말에 동의해. 모든 가족들이 함께 시간을 보낸다는 것은 좋은 거야.

| Vocabulary | taste 맛이 나다 | maybe 아마도 | plenty of 많은 | spend time 시간을 보내다 |

6

M Some banks charge fees to the customers. Do you think it's fair? I don't think so. Here at Eagle Bank, we don't charge you any fees. It is also easy to get a loan with our bank. Plus, our website is very easy to use. We always do our best for the satisfaction of our customers. So try Eagle Bank today.

남 어떤 은행들은 고객들에게 수수료를 청구합니다. 여러분은 이것이 정당하다고 생각합니까? 저는 그렇게 생각하지 않습니다. 우리 Eagle은행에서는, 여러분에게 그 어떤 수수료도 부과하지 않습니다. 또한 우리 은행에서는 대출을 받는 것도 쉽습니다. 게다가, 우리의 웹사이트는 사용하기에 편리합니다. 우리는 언제나 고객의 만족을 위해 최선을 다하고 있습니다. 그러니 오늘 Eagle은행을 이용해 보세요.

| Vocabulary | charge 요금을 부과하다 | fee 수수료, 요금 | fair 정당한 | loan 대출(금) | satisfaction 만족 | customer 고객 |

7

W Well, Mr. Moyer isn't holding a party this year for our class. What do you think of that, Harold?

여 음. Moyer선생님이 올해에는 우리 반을 위한 파티를 열지 않을 거래. 너는 그것에 대해 어떻게 생각해, Harold?

M I think <u>it</u> <u>makes</u> <u>sense</u>. I mean, I like the parties, but we need the money for <u>more</u> <u>important</u> <u>things</u> like donations for the poor, and so on.	**남** 나는 일리가 있다고 생각해. 내 말은 나는 파티를 좋아하지만, 우리는 그 돈을 가난한 사람들을 위한 기부와 같은 더 중요한 일에 사용해야 한다고 생각해.
W Sorry, but I'm <u>against</u> <u>it</u>. I mean, those parties are <u>a</u> <u>nice</u> <u>treat</u> for us. I believe that they make us relax <u>and</u> <u>be</u> <u>cheerful</u>.	**여** 미안하지만, 난 동의 할 수 없어. 내말은, 그러한 파티는 우리에게 제공되는 멋진 대접이잖아. 파티는 우리가 휴식을 취할 수 있도록 해주고 신나게 해주거든.
M Well, maybe we'll <u>get</u> <u>another</u> <u>one</u> next year.	**남** 음. 내년에는 우리에게 또 다른 파티가 있겠지 뭐.

Vocabulary	hold 열다, 개최하다 make sense 일리가 있다, 말이 되다 donation 기부 treat 대접 relax 휴식을 취하다

8

M Well, that wasn't too bad. <u>Do</u> <u>you</u> <u>think</u> my gums will be OK?	**남** 음. 그리 아프진 않았어요. 제 잇몸은 괜찮을까요?
W I think they will be OK. Your two teeth <u>came</u> <u>out</u> cleanly.	**여** 괜찮을 거에요. 이빨 두 개가 깨끗하게 빠져 나왔거든요.
M That's <u>good</u> <u>to</u> <u>hear</u>. Thanks for <u>pulling</u> <u>them</u> <u>out</u> for me, doctor.	**남** 그거 다행이네요. 제 이을 뽑아주셔서 감사해요, 의사선생님.
W Sure. Just take care of <u>your</u> <u>teeth</u> and gums.	**여** 물론이죠. 치아와 잇몸 관리만 잘하도록 하세요.

Vocabulary	gum 잇몸 come out (밖으로) 나오다 cleanly 깨끗하게 pull out 뽑다 take care of ~을 관리하다

UNIX WHICH IS SHORTER?

🌀 Check Up

01 c → a → b   **02** a, b

03 A I can't decide on a dress. <u>Which do you think</u> is better, <u>the red one or</u> the black one?

B <u>I think the red one</u> is better.

A Well, how about the shoes?

B The blue ones <u>look better on you</u>.

Check Up Scripts

01

W Hey, Mark, I heard that you're in a race after school today. I can't believe it!

M Yeah. I think I have a good chance at winning, though. There's only two other people racing.

W Jerry is racing with you, too, right, Mark?

M Yeah, and I'm faster than Jerry. But Dan is also racing, and he's faster than me.

여 이봐, Mark. 너 오늘 방과 후에 경주를 한다고 들었는데. 믿을 수가 없어!

남 응. 하지만 내가 승리할 수도 있을 것 같아. 선수가 두 명밖에 더 없거든.

여 Jerry도 너와 경주를 하지, 그렇지, Mark?

남 응, 내가 Jerry보다 빨라. 하지만 Dan도 경주를 하는데, 그가 나보다 빠르지.

Vocabulary	race 경주; 경주를 하다 chance 기회

02

M Which school do you think is better, West End Middle School or Pinewood Academy?

W Hmm. Pinewood has better teachers. I'd have to say that's a better school.

M That's surprising. You go to a public school. I thought you'd like a public school better.

W Yeah. But our school building became too old.

남 너는 West End 중학교와 Pinewood 아카데미 중에 어느 학교가 더 나은 것 같아?

여 흠. Pinewood에 더 실력 좋은 선생님들이 있잖아. 나는 Pinewood가 더 좋은 학교라고 할 수 있을 것 같아.

남 놀랍네. 너는 공립학교에 다니잖아. 난 네가 공립학교를 더 좋아 할 거라 생각했는데.

여 응. 하지만 학교 건물은 너무 오래 되었거든.

Vocabulary	middle school 중학교 academy 아카데미, 전문학교 public 공립의

03

A I can't decide on a dress. Which do you think is better, the red one or the black one?

B I think the red one is better.

A Well, how about the shoes?

B The blue ones look better on you.

A 난 드레스를 못 고르겠어. 넌 빨간 색과 검은색 중에 어떤 것이 더 나은 것 같니?

B 나는 빨간색이 더 나은 것 같아.

A 그럼, 신발은?

B 파란색이 너한테 더 잘 어울리는 것 같아.

Vocabulary	look better on ~에게 더 잘 어울리다

1

M Janice, I'm glad you could come to the party. Say, have you met my aunt?

W I don't think so. Is she here?

M Yeah, she's right over there. She's the woman with the red hair.

W Oh, do you mean that woman in the green dress?

M No, my aunt is shorter than that woman.

W Oh, I see her. She's wearing sunglasses, isn't she?

M Right.

남 Janice, 네가 파티에 올 수 있어서 기뻐. 근데 우리 이모 만난 적 있니?

여 없는 것 같아. 그녀가 이곳에 계시니?

남 응, 저쪽에 계셔. 붉은 머리를 하고 있는 여자분이셔.

여 오, 초록색 드레스를 입고 있는 여성 말이니?

남 아니, 우리 이모는 저 여성보다 키가 더 작아.

여 아, 보인다. 그녀는 선글라스를 쓰고 있어, 맞지?

남 그래.

Vocabulary	aunt 이모 wear 쓰다, 착용하다 sunglasses 선글라스

2

M Welcome to the Sandy Shore Vacation Resort. We hope you enjoy your stay here. There are several activities for the whole family. We have a hot spa, sauna, and gym for men and women. For children, we have many fun sports programs, like basketball training and miniature golf. And then there's the highlight of our resort – the beach! We have miles and miles of white sand and blue ocean! It's bigger than any other beach resort in the country. I'm sure that you will have a great time here!

남 Sandy 해변 휴양 리조트에 오신 것을 환영합니다. 우리는 여러분이 이곳에서 즐거운 시간을 보내시길 바랍니다. 온 가족을 위한 다양한 활동들이 준비되어 있습니다. 남성과 여성들을 위한 뜨거운 온천과 사우나, 그리고 헬스클럽이 마련되어 있습니다. 아이들을 위한 것으로는, 농구 교습과 미니골프와 같은 여러 재미있는 스포츠 프로그램들이 준비되어 있습니다. 그리고 우리 리조트의 하이라이트인 해변도 있습니다! 우리는 넓디 넓은 백사장과 푸른 해변을 가지고 있습니다! 이것은 국내의 다른 어떤 해변 리조트보다 크기가 큽니다. 저는 여러분이 이곳에서 즐거운 시간을 보내시리라는 것을 확신합니다!

Vocabulary	shore 해변 vacation resort 휴양 리조트 stay 체류, 방문 several 몇 가지의 spa 온천 gym 헬스클럽, 체육관 training 교습, 훈련 miniature 소형의, 축소된 highlight 하이라이트, 백미 white sand 백사장

3

W When I was younger, I dreamed of becoming a model. When I turned 14, I started growing taller. That got my hopes up. However, that was two years ago, and I've stopped growing now. I'm not very tall, so I gave up my dream. Then I was reading about this famous model. I'm actually a little

여 내가 어렸을 적에, 나는 모델이 되는 것을 꿈꾸었다. 내가 14살이 되었을 때, 나는 키가 자라기 시작했다. 그것이 나의 희망을 부풀렸다. 하지만, 그것은 2년 전이며, 나는 현재 성장이 멈추었다. 나는 그다지 키가 크지 않으며, 그래서 나는 내 꿈을 포기했었다. 그런데 나는 이 유명한 모델에 대한 글을 읽게 되었다. 나는 사실 그녀보다 약간 더 키가 크다! 믿을 수가 없다. 이것이 나의 희망을 되살려주었다.

taller than she is! It's incredible. This renews
my hope.

Question How old is the speaker now?

질문 화자는 지금 몇 살입니까?

dream of ~을 꿈꾸다, 바라다	turn (나이가) ~살이 되다
give up 포기하다	incredible 믿을 수가 없는, 놀라운
renew 되살리다	

4

M Excuse me, but I want to buy a new camera.
Which do you think is better, this film
camera or this digital camera?

W Well, the digital camera has many functions
that allow different kinds of effects, and it's
easier to send pictures to computers.

M Hmm. That is pretty nice. But I think that's
not my style. Do you have any other
models of digital cameras?

W Of course. Come follow me, and I'll show
them to you.

남 실례합니다만. 저는 새로운 카메라를 구매하고 싶어요.
이 필름 카메라와 디지털 카메라 중에 어떤 것이 더
나은 것 같으세요?

여 음. 이 디지털 카메라는 다양한 효과들을 가능하게 해주
는 많은 기능을 가지고 있고, 컴퓨터로 사진을 전송하기
에도 더 쉽습니다.

남 흠. 꽤 괜찮군요. 하지만 그것은 제 스타일이 아니네요.
디지털 카메라로 다른 모델이 있나요?

여 물론입니다. 저를 따라오세요, 보여드릴게요.

film camera 필름 카메라   function 기능   effect 효과   style 스타일, 취향

5

M Hey, I saw Melissa yesterday.

W Oh, really? I haven't spoken with her in
years! How is she doing?

M She's doing really well. She actually got a
full scholarship last month.

W Wow, I can't believe it! I didn't know she
was such a brilliant student.

M Yeah. But I think she deserves it because
she studies very hard.

W You're right.

남 이봐. 나 어제 Melisa를 보았어.

여 오, 정말? 나는 한동안 그녀와 이야기를 나누지 못했어!
그녀는 어떻게 지내니?

남 그녀는 잘 지내고 있어. 그녀는 사실 지난달에 전액
장학금을 받았어.

여 와우, 믿을 수가 없어! 나는 그녀가 그렇게 머리가 좋은
지 몰랐어.

남 맞아. 하지만 난 그녀가 그럴 자격이 있다고 생각해.
왜냐하면 그녀는 열심히 공부 하잖아.

여 네 말이 맞아.

scholarship 장학금   brillant 영리한   deserve ~할 자격이 있는

6

M Mary, when should we leave for our
spring vacation?

W I'm not sure. But April would be the best
time. Which do you think is better, the first
week or the second week?

M Hmm. A lot of people will take their breaks
during the first week of April.

남 Mary. 우리 봄 휴가를 언제 떠나는 게 좋을까?

여 잘 모르겠어. 하지만 4월 달이 가장 좋은 시기이기는 하
지. 첫째 주와 둘째 주 중에 언제가 더 좋아?

남 흠. 많은 사람들이 그들의 휴가를 4월 첫째 주에 떠날
거야.

W So a lot of them will return on the 6th and 7th. Why don't we leave the Thursday before that?

M Sounds great.

여 그러니 그들 대부분이 6일이나 7일에 돌아 올거야. 우리는 그 전날인 목요일에 떠나는 게 어때?

남 그거 좋은 생각이야.

take break 휴식을 취하다, 휴가를 떠나다

① M I hit two home runs in yesterday's baseball game!

W Really? That's amazing!

② W Which coffee do you think is better, the Sumatra or the Columbian blend?

M I think the Sumatra has a richer flavor.

③ M Which tie do you think is better, the red one or the striped one?

W I think that coat looks great on you.

④ W You know something? I'm shorter than my younger brother now.

M Wow! That's surprising. He grew up quickly.

⑤ M Did you hear that Ronald got all A's in school?

W I can't believe it. He didn't study hard this year.

① 남 나 어제 야구 경기에서 홈런을 쳤어!

여 정말? 멋지다!

② 여 너는 Sumatra와 Columbian blend중에 어떤 커피가 더 낫다고 생각하니?

남 나는 Sumatra가 더 풍부한 향을 가지고 있는 것 같아.

③ 남 너는 빨간 색과 줄무늬 중에 어떤 넥타이가 더 나은 것 같니?

여 내 생각에는 그 코트가 너에게 잘 어울리는 것 같아.

④ 여 너 그거 알아? 나는 이제 내 남동생보다 더 키가 작아.

남 와우! 대단하네. 그는 빨리 키가 자라는 구나.

⑤ 남 너 Ronald가 학교에서 전 과목 A를 받았다는 얘기 들었어?

여 말도 안돼. 그는 이번에 공부를 열심히 하지 않았는데.

home run 홈런   rich 풍부한   flavor (독특한) 풍미, 향미   striped 줄무늬의   grow up 성장하다

W Did you hear about Sally?

M No, I didn't. What happened to her?

W She helped the police catch a thief!

M Really? That's incredible! How did she do it?

W Well, she saw this guy trying to get into a car. So she told a policeman about it, and they found out that it was a thief. Then they took him to jail.

M That's good to hear.

여 Sally에 대해 들었니?

남 아니. 그녀에게 무슨 일이 있었는데?

여 그녀가 경찰이 도둑을 체포하는 것을 도와주었어!

남 정말? 대단하다! 그녀는 어떻게 그렇게 한 거야?

여 음. 그녀는 한 남자가 차 안으로 들어가려고 하는 걸 봤대. 그래서 그녀는 경찰에게 그 사실을 알렸고, 경찰은 그가 도둑이라는 것을 알았지. 그리고 경찰은 그 남자를 감옥에 넣었대.

남 잘됐구나.

thief 도둑, 절도범   incredible 굉장한   get into ~로 들어가다   jail 감옥

UNIT X DO YOU GET IT?

⚬ Check Up

01 c **02** has basketball practice.

03 A Hello? Mom, it's me. Can you tell me how to get to grandmother's house?

B OK, go west on Wilson Street, and turn right at the second block. <u>Did you get that?</u>

A <u>I'm sorry</u>, but <u>I didn't hear you</u>. <u>Can you repeat that please?</u>

B I said go west on Wilson Street, and turn right at the second block.

A I got it. Thank you.

Check Up Scripts

01

M They said we're going to have pretty bad weather tomorrow.

남 내일 날씨가 별로 좋지 않을 거래요.

W Would you say that again? I wasn't really paying attention.

여 다시 한 번 말해 줄래요? 집중을 안하고 있었어요.

M We're supposed to get some thunderstorms tomorrow.

남 내일 폭풍우가 올 거라고요.

W Oh, I was going to go fishing, but I'll have to cancel then.

여 오, 낚시 가려고 했는데, 취소해야 겠어요.

Vocabulary	pay attention ~에 집중하다 thunderstorm 폭풍우 cancel 취소하다

02

W I had a really fun time today, Ron.

여 오늘 정말 즐거웠어. Ron.

M Me, too. Say, do you know what time it is?

남 나도야. 근데 지금 몇 시인지 아니?

W Let's see. It's almost 9 o'clock.

여 어디 보자. 9시 다 되어가네.

M Almost nine? Oh, sorry. I must be off. I have to get up early tomorrow for basketball practice.

남 9시가 다 되어간다고? 오, 미안해. 나 가봐야겠어. 나 내일 농구 연습이 있어서 아침 일찍 일어나야 하거든.

W That's fine. See you.

여 알겠어. 다음에 보자.

03

A Hello? Mom, it's me. Can you tell me how to get to grandmother's house?

A 여보세요? 엄마. 저에요. 할머니 댁까지 어떻게 가야 하는지 알려주시겠어요?

B OK, go west on Wilson Street, and turn right at the second block. Did you get it?

B 그래. Wilson도로에서 서쪽으로 가다가, 두 번째 골목에서 오른쪽으로 꺾으면 돼. 이해했니?

A I'm sorry, but I didn't hear you. Can you repeat that please?

A 죄송하지만 안 들렸어요. 다시 한번 말씀해 주시겠어요?

B I said go west on Wilson Street, and turn right at the second block.

B Wilson도로에서 서쪽으로 가다가, 두 번째 골목에서 오른쪽으로 꺾으면 된다고 했단다.

A I got it. Thank you.

A 알겠어요. 감사해요.

1

M Hey, Mary, can you tell me where the mall is? I need to get there right away.

W Yeah. You know where the post office is? Well, north of that is Hilton Road. Just turn left on Hilton Road and turn right at the first light. After the right turn, pass over the highway. The mall is on the other side. Do you get it?

M Yes, I got it. Thanks.

남 있잖아. Mary, 쇼핑몰이 어디에 있는지 알려줄래? 나 지금 그곳에 가야 해.

여 그래. 우체국 어디에 있는지 알지? 음. 우체국 북쪽에 Hilton 거리가 있어. 그곳에서 좌회전해서 첫 번째 신호등에서 우회전 해. 우회전 하고 나서 고속도로를 건너. 쇼핑몰이 맞은편에 있거든. 이해했니?

남 응. 이해했어. 고마워.

| Vocabulary | right away 지금, 당장   north 북쪽   pass over ~을 지나가다 |

2

[The answering machine beeps.]

W Hi, Curtis, this is Jessica. I was calling to tell you about my party next Thursday. My parents said I could invite five of my friends, so I'm asking you. Oh, I'm sorry, but I have to go now. My mom needs my help with something. Please call me back.

[자동응답기 소리]

여 안녕, Curtis, 나 Jessica야. 다음주 목요일에 있을 내 파티에 대해 얘기하려고 전화했어. 부모님이 친구 5명을 초대해도 좋다고 하셔서 너한테 물어보는 거야. 오. 미안하지만 지금 가봐야겠어. 엄마가 도와달라고 하셔서. 나에게 전화 줘.

| Vocabulary | invite 초대하다 |

3

[The telephone rings.]

M Hello?

W Hey, Jacob. It's Jane.

M Where were you, Jane? I thought we were going to see a movie this afternoon.

W I'm sorry, I didn't hear you. It's really noisy on this train.

M I asked where you were.

W Oh. I went to visit my grandmother. She wanted to have lunch. It happened suddenly. I'm so sorry.

M That's OK. Never mind.

[전화벨 소리]

남 여보세요?

여 Jacob. 나 Jane이야.

남 너 어디에 있었어. Jane? 우리 오후에 영화보기로 했었잖아.

여 미안하지만. 못 들었어. 이 기차 안이 너무 시끄러워.

남 너 어디에 있었냐고 물었어.

여 오. 우리 할머니를 뵈러 갔었어. 할머니께서 점심을 함께 하길 원하셨어. 갑자기 약속이 잡혔어. 정말 미안해.

남 괜찮아. 너무 신경 쓰지마.

| Vocabulary | happen 일어나다   suddenly 갑자기 |

4

[The telephone rings.]	[전화벨 소리]
W Hello, this is Dr. Stevens' office. How can I help you?	여 여보세요, Stevens 선생님의 병원입니다. 도와드릴까요?
M Hi, this is Larry Butler. I need to schedule an appointment this week with Dr. Stevens.	남 안녕하세요. Larry Butler입니다. 이번 주에 Stevens 선생님과의 진료 일정을 잡고 싶어요.
W Yes, sir. Let's see. We have two spots available. One is for 3:00 p.m. on Tuesday. The other is for 1:00 p.m. on Friday.	여 알겠습니다. 어디 보자. 두 자리가 비네요. 하나는 화요일 오후 3시이고, 다른 하나는 금요일 오후 1시입니다.
M Sorry. Could you repeat that again?	남 죄송합니다. 다시 한번 말씀해 주시겠어요?
W You can come in at 3:00 p.m. on Tuesday or 1:00 p.m. on Friday.	여 화요일 오후 3시에 오셔도 되고, 금요일 오후 1시에 오셔도 됩니다.
M Well, Friday would be fine with me.	남 음. 금요일이 좋을 것 같군요.
W Okay, sir.	여 알겠습니다.

> **Vocabulary** schedule 일정을 짜다 appointment 약속, 예약 spot 자리 available 시간이 있는, 여유가 있는

5

M Good afternoon, ma'am. Where can I take you today?	남 좋은 오후입니다. 부인. 어디로 모실까요?
W The First National Bank, please.	여 First 국립은행으로 가주세요.
M I'm sorry, I didn't hear you. Where was that again?	남 죄송하지만, 못 들었습니다. 어디라고 하셨죠?
W The First National Bank. And please hurry.	여 First 국립은행이라고 했어요. 서둘러주세요.
M All right. I'll try. But there was an accident ahead. We'll have to take another road.	남 알겠습니다. 노력해볼게요. 하지만 앞에 사고가 있었어요. 다른 길로 가야 할 것 같아요.
W Fine. Just get there as quickly as possible, please.	여 알겠어요. 가능한 빨리만 가주세요.

> **Vocabulary** accident 사고 ahead 앞에 quickly 빠르게 possible 가능한

6

M How have you enjoyed the evening, Leslie?	남 오늘 저녁 어땠어. Leslie?
W It's been really nice. Hold on a second. My phone is going off. I just got a message.	여 정말 좋았어. 잠깐만. 내 전화가 울리고 있어. 문자가 왔네.
M Is something wrong?	남 무슨 문제 있어?
W I'm sorry, but I must go now. That was my roommate. Our apartment has been robbed. She just found out.	여 미안하지만 나 지금 가봐야겠어. 내 룸메이트야. 우리 아파트에 도둑이 들었어. 그녀가 방금 알았나 봐.
M Oh, I'm sorry. Of course you should go.	남 오, 어떡해. 물론 가봐야지.

> **Vocabulary** go off (전화, 알람 등이) 울리다 rob 도둑질하다

W Oh, it's so hard to buy clothes with so little money.

M Well, why don't you try a flea market?

W Sorry. Would you say that again, please?

M A flea market. You know, it's where people sell and buy things at almost half price. You could get some good items from one of those.

W Maybe. But I don't know where or when they're held.

M I'll show you a website that can help you.

Vocabulary	flea market 벼룩시장　half 절반의　held (모임 등을) 열다. 개최하다.　create 새로 만들다. 창조하다.

여 오, 적은 돈으로 옷들을 사 입기가 너무 힘들어.

남 흠. 벼룩시장에 가보는 게 어때?

여 미안해. 다시 한번만 말해줄래?

남 벼룩시장. 왜 있잖아, 사람들이 물건을 거의 반 가격에 사고 팔고 하는 곳 말이야. 그런 곳에서 너는 좋은 물건들을 얻을 수 있을 거야.

여 아마도. 하지만 어디서 언제 열리는지 나는 몰라.

남 너에게 도움이 될만한 웹사이트를 하나 소개해줄게.

M Mr. Lawrence, I'm writing this e-mail to ask about today's announcement. You told us when the school picnic would be. Could you tell me again? I'm sorry, I didn't hear you. The student next to me kept whispering to me. I just want to make sure I can make it to the picnic. I might be going to Philadelphia with my family on that day. Thanks.

Vocabulary	announcement 발표(내용), 소식　next to ~의 옆에　keep -ing ~을 계속하다　whisper 소근거리다. 귓속말을 하다 make sure 확실히 하다

남 Lawrence선생님, 저는 오늘 있었던 공지에 관해 궁금한 사항이 있어 메일 드려요. 저희 학교 소풍이 언제 있을지 말씀해 주셨는데요. 다시 한번 말씀해 주시겠어요? 경청하지 못해 죄송해요. 제 옆에 있던 학생이 계속해서 귓속말을 했어요. 저는 소풍을 갈 수 있을지 없을지 확인을 하고 싶어요. 그 날에 가족들과 함께 필라델피아에 가게 될지도 모르거든요. 감사합니다.

UNIT XI HAVE YOU EVER SEEN IT?

Check Up

p.67

01 b

02

	Jill	Bryan
golf	✓	
basketball		
soccer		✓

03 **A** Have you ever tried to eat a whole pizza at once?

B Yes, I have. It made me really sick. I've also tried eating a whole chicken. Have you?

A No, I haven't.

Check Up Scripts

01

M Say, have you ever met my friend Matt?

W Yes, I have. He's got thick glasses, right?

M Well, not anymore. He got contact lenses recently. Also, he shaved his head.

W Oh, really? That's a big change. I probably wouldn't recognize him if I saw him now.

남 너 내 친구 Matt 만나본 적 있니?

여 응, 있어. 그는 두꺼운 안경을 쓰고 있어. 그렇지?

남 음, 이제 아니야. 최근에 콘택트렌즈를 장만했거든. 그리고, 머리도 밀었어.

여 오 정말이야? 정말 큰 변화구나. 내가 지금 그를 보게 된다면 아마도 알아보지 못할 거야.

Vocabulary	anymore 이제는, 더 이상은 contact lenses 콘택트렌즈 recently 최근에 shave 밀어버리다, 털을 깎다 probably 아마도 recognize 알아보다

02

W Guess what, Brian? I'm going to see a soccer game next month! Two teams from Britain are playing each other in a special match.

M Cool. Have you ever played soccer before, Jill?

W No, I haven't. The only sport I play is golf. What about you?

M I play soccer all the time. I just never go to games, though.

여 너 그거 아니, Brian? 나 다음 달에 축구 경기를 보러 갈 거야! 영국출신의 두 팀이 스페셜 경기를 펼칠 거야.

남 멋지다. 너도 축구를 해본 적 있니, Jill?

여 아니, 없어. 내가 하는 유일한 스포츠는 골프야. 너는 어떠니?

남 나는 언제나 축구를 해. 하지만 경기를 보러 가지는 않아.

Vocabulary	Britain 영국 usually 대개

03

A Have you ever tried to eat a whole pizza at once?

B Yes, I have. It made me really sick. I've also tried eating a whole chicken. Have you?

A No, I haven't.

A 너 한번에 피자 한판 먹어보려고 한 적 있니?

B 응, 있어. 속이 엄청 안 좋았어. 나는 치킨 한 마리도 먹으려고 한 적이 있었어. 너도 그런 적 있니?

A 나는 없어.

Actual Test   1 ③   2 ①   3 ③   4 ④   5 ②   6 ②   7 ①   8 ④ | p.68

M Have you ever seen one of these? They are like clouds, but they reach from the sky to the ground. They also spin around very quickly. This is because dangerous wind from a storm is causing them. They can destroy lots of buildings. If you see one, you are in great danger. Hide, and get away from any windows immediately!

남 당신은 이러한 것들을 본적이 있습니까? 이것들은 구름처럼 생겼지만 하늘에서 지면까지 내려옵니다. 그것들은 굉장히 빠르게 회전하기도 합니다. 이것은 폭풍으로 인한 위험한 바람이 그것들을 만들어내기 때문입니다. 그것들은 여러 빌딩을 파괴할 수 있습니다. 여러분이 이것을 보게 된다면 굉장한 위험에 처한 것이니. 즉시 몸을 숨기고, 창문으로부터 멀리 떨어지세요!

Vocabulary | reach 이르다   spin 회전하다   dangerous 위험한   storm 폭풍   cause 야기하다. 초래하다   destroy 파괴하다   in danger 위험에 처한   get away 달아나다   immediately 즉시

2

M Hey, Karen. Have you ever tried this yoga pose before?

W Let's see. Yes, I have. It can be a little difficult at first.

M How do you do it?

W Well, the first thing you do is put your hands together, like this. Then you raise your arms up high over your head. Finally, stand on just your right leg. Then bring your left foot up to your right knee.

M Ah, I think I got it now. Thanks.

남 안녕. Karen. 너는 이 요가 자세를 해 본 적이 있니?

여 어디 보자. 응, 있어. 처음에는 조금 어려울 수도 있어.

남 어떻게 하는 건데?

여 처음에 네가 할 일은 두 손을 모으는 거야. 이렇게. 그 다음 팔을 머리 위로 높게 들어. 마지막으로 오른쪽 다리로만 서 있어. 그리고 너의 왼쪽 발을 네 오른쪽 무릎에 갖다 대는 거야.

남 아. 이제 알 것 같아. 고마워.

Vocabulary | pose 자세   difficult 어려운   put together 모으다   raise up ~을 위로 올리다   knee 무릎

M Have you ever put a lot of time and care into a creative project, Penny?

W Yes, I have. I recently finished a painting. I've been working on it for months now.

M You must really enjoy your artwork.

W I do. It helps me relax. And it lets me use my imagination.

남 Penny. 너는 창의적인 프로젝트에 시간과 관심을 쏟은 적이 있니?

여 응. 있어. 나는 최근에 그림을 한 점 완성했어. 난 몇 달째 그 작업을 해왔거든.

남 내 생각에 너는 정말로 너의 작품 활동을 즐기는 거 같아.

여 맞아. 작품 활동은 나를 안정시켜줘. 그리고 나의 상상력을 발휘하게 해주지.

4

W Mr. Green sure is amazing!

M Uh, who is Mr. Green?

W He works at the security office. He's about the same age as my grandfather. And he has some really cool stories!

M Really? Like what?

W Well, he served in both the Korean and Vietnam Wars. He was also a police officer in New York. Haven't you ever spoken with him?

여 Green씨는 정말 멋진 것 같아!

남 어, Green씨가 누구야?

여 그는 경비실에서 일하시는 분이야. 그는 나의 할아버지와 연세가 같아. 그리고 정말 재미있는 이야기를 많이 알고 있으시지.

남 정말? 어떤 이야기?

여 음, 그는 한국전쟁과 월남전쟁에 참전했었어. 그는 뉴욕에서 경찰관으로도 근무를 했었어. 너는 그와 이야기를 나누어 본 적이 없니?

5

W Devon, you've gone on lots of vacations, right?

M Yeah, I guess so.

W Have you ever gone on a cruise ship before?

M Yes, I have. A few times. Why do you ask?

W Well, I am thinking of going on one with my parents. Is it worth the price?

M I think so. You get to see all kinds of nice islands and beaches. You can also do all kinds of fun things on the ship itself. They're usually nicer than most hotels!

W Really? That's interesting. Thank you.

여 Devon, 너는 휴가를 많이 떠났었어, 그렇지?

남 응, 그런 것 같아.

여 너는 유람선 여행을 가본적도 있니?

남 응, 있어. 몇 번. 왜 물어보는 거야?

여 음. 부모님이랑 한번 가보려고 하거든. 가격만큼 가치가 있니?

남 그런 것 같아. 여러 개의 멋진 섬과 해변을 볼 수 있어. 배 위에서도 여러 가지 재미있는 것들을 할 수 있고 말이야. 대개 유람선이 대부분의 호텔보다 더 나아!

여 정말? 그거 재미있겠네. 고마워.

6

W Hey, Shelly. I haven't talked with you in a while. I was just sending this e-mail to see how you were doing. Also, I posted a link to the Fine Arts Academy of Hartford on here. Have you ever heard of this place? It teaches people how to sing, act, dance, and play music! You know my lifelong dream is to appear on the show *American Idol* someday. Maybe these people can help me with that.

여 이봐, Shelly. 내가 한동안 너와 이야기를 못한 것 같아. 네가 잘 지내고 있는지 안부를 물으려고 이메일을 쓰고 있어. 그리고, Hartford의 예술 아카데미로 연결되는 링크를 걸어놨어. 너 이곳에 대해 들어본 적 있니? 그곳에서는 사람들에게 노래, 연기, 춤, 그리고 음악을 연주하는 법을 가르쳐 준다고! 나의 평생의 꿈이 언젠가는 「아메리칸 아이돌」 쇼에 출연하는 것이란 걸 너도 알잖아. 아마도 그들은 그렇게 되도록 도와줄 거야.

7

W Hey, Billy. I have a question.

M What is it?

W Have you ever seen a flying saucer?

M No, I haven't. I thought I did once. But that was back when I was a kid. It was just a plane.

W Oh. Do you think aliens are real?

M I really don't know.

W What if they are real? Would you be scared?

M Look, I'm really busy right now. Can we talk about this later?

여 있잖아, Billy. 질문이 있어.

남 뭔데?

여 너 비행접시 본 적 있니?

남 아니, 없어. 난 본 적이 있다고 생각했어. 그런데 그땐 내가 어렸어. 그건 그냥 비행기였을 뿐이야.

여 오. 너는 외계인이 진짜라고 생각하니?

남 모르겠어.

여 그들이 진짜라면? 넌 두려울 것 같니?

남 이봐, 난 지금 정말 바쁘다고. 나중에 얘기하면 안되겠어?

Vocabulary   flying saucer 비행접시, UFO   alien 외계인   real 진짜의

8

M Wendy, I have a problem.

W What is it?

M Well, have you ever been in love with someone who didn't love you?

W Yes, I have. It hurts a lot. Is that what's wrong?

M Yeah. There's this girl in my chemistry class who is amazing. But I don't think she even notices me. I want to ask her out, but I'm too nervous!

W Gee, that's rough. But you should at least try. Otherwise, you'll never know for sure!

남 Wendy, 나에게 문제가 생겼어.

여 뭔데?

남 음. 너는 너를 사랑하지 않는 사람을 사랑한적이 있니?

여 응. 있어. 너무 아프지. 그게 무슨 문제가 있니?

남 응. 내 화학 수업에 멋진 여자애가 있거든. 하지만 그녀는 나를 알지도 못해. 나는 그녀에게 데이트 신청을 하고 싶은데, 너무 떨려!

여 이런, 곤란하겠다. 하지만 시도는 해봐야지. 그렇지 않고서는 너는 절대 확실하게 알지 못해!

Vocabulary   be in love with ~를 사랑하다   chemistry 화학   notice 알아차리다   ask somebody out ~에게 데이트 신청을 하다
nervous 불안해하는, 걱정하는   at least 적어도   otherwise 그렇지 않으면   for sure 확실히, 분명히   break up 헤어지다

UNIT XII CHEER UP!

✿ Check Up

01 b **02** a

03 A Good luck on today's English test.

B Thanks. I wish you well, too.

[two hours later]

A How was your test?

B I think I failed again.

A Cheer up. You can take it next month. You'll do better next time.

Check Up Scripts

01

M Well, I'm so glad I met you here, Cathy.

W Me, too.

M By the way, will you come to this camp again next year?

W I don't think so. It's too bad we have to part like this. We should hang out sometime.

M That sounds good. Please keep in touch. God bless you.

남 음. 널 여기서 만나게 되어 너무 좋아. Cathy.

여 나도 그래.

남 그나저나. 너 내년에도 이 캠프에 참가 할 거니?

여 안 할 것 같아. 이렇게 헤어지다니 아쉬워. 우리 언제 한 번 보자.

남 좋은 생각이야. 연락하고 지내자. 행운이 함께하길 바래.

Vocabulary	part 헤어지다 keep in touch 연락하다

02

W Well, today I'm singing in a big contest at a famous talent agency.

M Oh, really? I didn't know you wanted to become a singer.

W Of course. My favorite singer is Britney Spears, and I want to be famous just like her.

M That's cool. Good luck on your performance. I'll keep my fingers crossed for you.

여 음, 나 오늘 유명한 연예 기획사에서 주최하는 큰 경연에서 노래할거야.

남 오, 정말? 난 네가 가수가 되고 싶어하는지 몰랐어.

여 물론이지. 내가 가장 좋아하는 가수는 Britney Spears 인데. 난 그녀처럼 유명해지고 싶어.

남 멋지구나. 노래 잘 해. 행운을 빌어줄게.

Vocabulary	talent agency 연예 기획사 famous 유명한 performance 공연

03

A Good luck on today's English test.

B Thanks. I wish you well, too.

[*two hours later*]

A How was your test?

B I think I failed again.

A 오늘 영어시험 잘 봐.

B 고마워. 너도 잘 보길 바래.

[두 시간 뒤]

A 시험 어땠어?

B 나 또 떨어진 것 같아.

A Cheer up. You can take it next month. You'll do better next time.

A 기운 내. 다음달에도 시험 볼 수 있잖아. 다음 번에는 더 잘 할 거야.

| Vocabulary | fail (시험 등에서) 떨어지다, 실패하다 |

Actual Test　　1 ②　2 ②　3 ③　4 ①　5 ②　6 ④　7 ⑤　8 ④　　| p.74

① **M** I hope you do well on this test.

　W Thanks. I wish you luck, too.

② **M** I hope everything goes well in your new life together.

　W Thanks, Uncle Bob! And thanks for coming to the wedding.

③ **M** Well, I'm going to try to beat my best swimming time.

　W I'll keep my fingers crossed for you.

④ **M** That book I wanted wasn't at the bookstore.

　W Cheer up. Here, you can borrow my copy.

⑤ **M** Good luck. You'll need it on this slope.

　W Yeah. I'm not sure I can ski this well.

① 남　네가 이번 시험을 잘 봤으면 좋겠어.

　여　고마워. 너도 잘 보길 빌어.

② 남　함께 새로이 시작하는 삶에 있어 모든 것이 잘 풀렸으면 좋겠구나.

　여　고마워요, Bob 삼촌! 그리고 저희 결혼식에 와주셔서 감사해요.

③ 남　음, 나는 최고 수영시간 기록을 깨기 위해 노력할 거야.

　여　너를 위해 행운을 빌어줄게.

④ 남　내가 원하던 책이 서점에 없었어.

　여　기운 내. 여기, 내 책을 빌려줄게.

⑤ 남　행운을 빌어. 너는 슬로프에서 그게 필요할거야.

　여　맞아. 이번 슬로프에서 스키를 잘 탈 수 있을지 모르겠어.

| Vocabulary | beat 기록을 깨다　bookstore 서점　slope 슬로프, 경사지 |

2

W Dear Max,

I heard that your football team made it to the championship game next weekend. That's incredible! Good luck! I wish I could fly out there to see you. Unfortunately, I have a big business meeting next weekend, so I can't. Still, I'll be cheering for you. Take care!

Sincerely,

Aunt Glenda

여　Max에게,

너의 미식축구 팀이 다음 주말에 결승전에 진출한다고 들었어. 멋지구나! 행운을 빈다! 나도 가서 너를 보고 싶어. 안타깝게도, 나에게는 다음주에 중요한 업무 회의가 있어서, 갈 수가 없어. 하지만, 너를 응원할게. 건강하거라!

Glenda 이모가

| Vocabulary | football 미식축구　championship game 결승전　incredible 믿을 수 없을 만큼 놀라운　unfortunately 불행하게도, 안타깝게도 |

3

M Hey, Patty. How's it going?

W I'm doing okay. How are you doing, Steven?

M Alright. I'm actually preparing to take the entrance exam tomorrow.

W Really? Did you decide where you want to go to school?

M Not really. I want to see how I do on the test first before I start looking around.

W Well, good luck on your exam.

남 이봐, Patty. 잘 지내?

여 잘 지내. 너는 어떻게 지내, Steven?

남 괜찮아. 난 사실 내일 볼 입학시험을 준비하고 있어.

여 정말? 너는 어느 학교로 가고 싶은지 결정한 거야?

남 딱히 그렇진 않아. 알아보기 전에 내가 시험을 어떻게 치는지 보려고.

여 음, 시험 잘 보길 빌어.

> **Vocabulary**   entrance exam 입학시험   look around 돌아다니다, 알아보다

4

W This is just great.

M What's wrong, Claudia?

W The two guitarists in my rock band don't want to play together anymore. So our band has broken up.

M Oh, too bad. But look on the bright side. Now you can start your own band. You've always wanted to do that, right?

W Yeah. I still liked playing with those guys, though.

M Well, maybe some of them will still play with you.

여 이거 정말 잘된 일이군.

남 무슨 일이야, Claudia?

여 우리 록 밴드에서 두 명의 기타리스트가 더 이상 우리와 함께 연주를 하고 싶지 않대. 그래서 우리 밴드가 해체되었어.

남 오, 그거 안됐구나. 하지만 긍정적으로 생각해. 이제 너는 너만의 밴드를 시작할 수 있잖아. 너는 항상 그걸 바래 왔잖아, 안 그래?

여 응. 하지만 나는 그 멤버들과 계속 연주를 하고 싶단 말이야.

남 음. 아마도 멤버들 중 몇 명은 너와 함께 연주를 계속 하고 싶어할 수도 있어.

> **Vocabulary**   break up 해체되다

5

M You look kind of sad, Martha. What's the matter?

W I just got back from visiting my mom in the hospital.

M Oh, no! Is she okay?

W She's recovering from a heart attack. She's doing better. But she's still really sick.

M I'm sorry to hear that. I hope she gets well soon.

남 슬퍼 보이네, Martha. 무슨 일 있니?

여 병원에 계신 엄마를 뵙고 오는 중이야.

남 오 그럴수가! 그녀는 괜찮으셔?

여 심근경색인데 회복 중이셔. 더 나아지시긴 했어. 하지만 그녀는 아직도 많이 아프셔.

남 안됐구나. 그녀가 빨리 회복되셨으면 좋겠어.

> **Vocabulary**   recover 회복하다   heart attack 심장마비, 심근경색   get well 건강을 회복하다

6

M Hey, Sara. I heard that you're going to audition <u>for</u> a <u>role</u> in a movie. I know that you've wanted <u>to</u> <u>be</u> <u>an</u> <u>actress</u> for a long time. This will be a good chance for you. I've always <u>supported</u> <u>you</u>, and I know you'll do great <u>in</u> <u>your</u> <u>audition</u>.

남 있지, Sara. 네가 영화 속 배역으로 오디션을 보러 간다고 들었어. 난 네가 오랫동안 배우가 되고 싶어했다는 걸 알아. 이번이 너에게는 좋은 기회일거야. 나는 언제나 너를 지지해 왔고, 나는 네가 오디션에서 잘 할거라는걸 알아.

Vocabulary	audition 오디션　　role 역할　　support 지지하다, 지원하다　　silly 어리석은

7

W So, how did my test results <u>turn</u> <u>out</u>?

여 그래서, 제 검사 결과는 어떻게 나왔나요?

M They're okay, but your blood pressure is <u>a</u> <u>little</u> <u>high</u>, Martha. You need to <u>bring</u> <u>it</u> <u>down</u> before it becomes dangerous.

남 괜찮아, 하지만 혈압이 약간 높아, Martha. 위험해지기 전에 혈압을 낮춰야 해.

W Oh, this is terrible. I don't want <u>to</u> <u>get</u> <u>sick</u>!

여 오, 큰일이네요. 저는 아프고 싶지 않아요!

M <u>Cheer</u> <u>up</u>. Just eat healthy foods and exercise more. <u>That</u> <u>should</u> <u>lower</u> your blood pressure.

남 기운내. 몸에 좋은 음식을 먹고 운동을 좀 더 해. 그러면 혈압이 낮아질 거야.

W Okay. Thanks.

여 알겠어요. 감사합니다.

Vocabulary	test result 검사 결과　　turn out 판명되다, 밝혀지다　　blood pressure 혈압　　bring down 낮추다, 줄이다 dangerous 위험한　　at least 적어도　　healthy 건강에 좋은　　exercise 운동하다　　lower 낮추다, 내리다

8

M Well, it looks like Jack Pearson is going to be <u>the</u> <u>town's</u> <u>new</u> <u>mayor</u>.

남 음, Jack Pearson이 도시의 새로운 시장이 되나 보구나.

W I can't believe he won the election.

여 난 그가 선거에서 승리를 했다는 걸 믿을 수가 없어요.

M Well, he might not be that bad.

남 음, 그는 그렇게 나쁘지 않을 거란다.

W What are you talking about? He didn't know <u>how</u> <u>to</u> <u>run</u> his own company. How well can he run the town? Things <u>will</u> <u>be</u> <u>terrible</u>.

여 무슨 말씀이세요? 그는 자신의 기업도 어떻게 운영하는지 몰랐어요. 그런 그가 얼마나 도시를 잘 운영하겠어요? 모든 것이 엉망진창이 될 거에요.

M Look on the bright side. <u>We're</u> <u>moving</u> to a new town in a few months. You won't have to <u>worry</u> <u>about</u> <u>him</u>.

남 긍정적으로 생각해라. 우리는 몇 달 안에 다른 도시로 이사를 갈 거잖니. 그에 대해 너무 신경 쓰지 말거라.

W Yeah, I guess you're right.

여 그래요, 아빠 생각이 맞는 것 같아요.

Vocabulary	mayor 시장　　election 선거　　run 운영하다　　move 이사하다

모의고사 1회

01 ④	02 ①	03 ⑤	04 ③	05 ③	06 ⑤	07 ②	08 ①	09 ③	10 ②
11 ③	12 ③	13 ①	14 ④	15 ⑤	16 ④	17 ①	18 ④	19 ⑤	20 ②

01

M Long ago, people used to live in these buildings. They were very large, and they were usually made out of stone or brick. These buildings were very well protected, too. They had to be. The people who owned these buildings were usually nobles, queens, or kings. Their enemies would often attack these buildings. Most of these buildings have disappeared now.

남 오래 전에, 사람들은 이러한 건물에서 살았습니다. 이것들은 굉장히 컸으며, 주로 돌이나 벽돌로 만들어졌습니다. 이러한 건물들은 경호도 굉장히 잘 되어 있었습니다. 그것들은 그래야 했습니다. 이런 건물들을 소유한 사람들은 대부분 귀족이나 여왕 또는 왕이었습니다. 그들의 적이 이러한 건물들을 공격하곤 했습니다. 이러한 건물들의 대부분이 현재는 사라지고 없습니다.

02

W Guess who just won a new bike? Me!

M Really? You won a new bike? That's so cool! How did you do it?

W I won this speech contest last night at school. First prize was a ten-speed bike. And it's just the one I've always wanted, too!

M Congratulations.

여 새로운 자전거를 누가 받게 됐는지 아니? 나야!

남 정말? 네가 새로운 자전거를 상품으로 받았어? 정말 멋지다! 어떻게 한 거야?

여 어제 밤 학교에서 열린 말하기 대회에서 우승했거든. 1등 상품이 10단 변속 자전거였어. 내가 항상 가지고 싶어했던 것이기도 해!

남 축하해.

03

W Chester, I need your help with something.

M Sure. What is it, Mom?

W Well, I want to set up a profile for this social network. The page tells how to do it. But I don't get it. Could you set it up for me?

M Okay, I'll see what I can do.

여 Chester, 네 도움이 필요하구나.

남 물론이죠. 무슨 일이에요, 엄마?

여 음. 나는 이 소셜 네트워크에 프로필을 등록하고 싶어. 페이지에 어떻게 해야 하는지 나와는 있어. 그런데 이해가 안 되는구나. 네가 대신 등록해주겠니?

남 알겠어요, 제가 확인해보도록 할게요.

04

[The telephone rings.]

M Hello, this is the Clairmont Hotel. How can I help you?

[전화벨 소리]

남 여보세요, Clairmont 호텔입니다. 무엇을 도와드릴까요?

W	Hi, my name is Becky Foss. I'd like to reserve one of your largest rooms for five nights from January 16th to January 20th.	여	안녕하세요, 제 이름은 Becky Foss 입니다. 저는 1월 16일부터 1월 20일까지 가장 큰 방들 중 하나를 5일 동안 예약하고 싶어요.
M	All right. We have one available for that time. Now, our largest rooms are for $200 a night.	남	알겠습니다. 그 시기에 방 하나가 이용 가능합니다. 가장 큰 방은 하루 밤에 200달러입니다.
W	Okay, but I have a membership card at your hotel. I should get a discount, right?	여	네, 하지만 저는 당신 호텔의 회원카드를 가지고 있어요. 할인을 받을 수 있는 거죠?
M	Yes, ma'am. There is a 20% discount.	남	네, 부인. 20%의 할인을 받으실 수 있습니다.
W	That's great.	여	그거 좋군요.

05

M	Carrie, can you work for me next Thursday night? I'll work for you on Saturday morning.	남	Carrie, 다음 주 목요일 저녁에 나 대신 일해줄 수 있니? 내가 토요일 아침에 대신 일을 할게.
W	Uh, sorry, I can't. I have other plans.	여	오, 미안하지만 안돼. 나에게는 다른 계획이 있어.
M	Oh, no! Christina Aguilera is finally going to have a concert here next Thursday night! I've wanted to see her for a long time now.	남	오, 이런! 크리스티나 아길레라가 마침내 다음 주 목요일 밤에 이곳에서 콘서트를 연단 말이야! 나는 오랫동안 그녀를 보고 싶어 했는데.
W	I'm sorry, but maybe Rex can help you.	여	미안해. 하지만 Rex가 네 부탁을 들어줄 수 있을거야.

06

W	Oh, I'm so hungry! I wish I hadn't skipped lunch.	여	오, 나 너무 배가 고파! 점심을 거르지 말았어야 했는데.
M	Do you have a snack or something?	남	간식이나 다른 먹을거를 가지고 있니?
W	Nah. And I don't have any money to get a snack.	여	아니. 간식을 살 돈이 한 푼도 없어.
M	You know, I keep some energy bars in my desk. Would you like one?	남	있잖아, 내 책상에 에너지 바가 좀 있어. 하나 먹을래?
W	Oh, yes. Thanks so much.	여	오, 그래. 너무 고마워.

07

M	Okay. I'm dressed and ready to go. How about you, Jessica?	남	좋아. 나는 옷도 다 입었고 출발 할 준비가 됐어. 너는 어때, Jessica?
W	I'm ready, too. I've wanted to see tonight's play for a long time.	여	나도 준비가 되었어. 나는 오랫동안 오늘의 연극을 보고 싶었어.
M	Oh, hey, yesterday I noticed that the car needed some gas. We'll have to make a quick stop before we go to the train station.	남	오, 이봐. 어제 보니까 차에 기름을 넣어야겠더라고. 기차역에 가기 전에 주유소에 잠깐 들러야겠어.
W	Sure, but we have to make sure to catch that 7:15 train.	여	그래, 하지만 7시15분 기차를 타야 한다는 걸 명심해.

08

W Washington D.C. is a wonderful place to visit! It's the capital of the United States, so it has many tourist attractions. You can see several buildings built for well-known presidents, including George Washington, Thomas Jefferson, and Abraham Lincoln. You can also visit Arlington National Cemetery, where soldiers are buried. There is also the Smithsonian Museum. You can also take a tour of the White House.

여 워싱턴 D.C.는 방문하기에 멋진 장소입니다! 이곳은 미국의 수도이기도 하며, 굉장히 많은 관광지를 가지고 있습니다. 여러분은 조지 워싱턴, 토마스 제퍼슨, 아브라함 링컨을 포함한 유명한 대통령들을 위해 지어진 다양한 건물들을 볼 수 있습니다. 여러분은 군인들이 안장되어 있는 알링턴 국민묘지도 방문하실 수 있습니다. 스미스소니언 박물관도 있습니다. 여러분은 백악관도 둘러보실 수 있습니다.

09

M Well, I've had a good time today. You want to play one more set?

W I don't know. I think another couple wants to use this court.

M Well, I think those guys over there are about to leave. The couple waiting can take that court. Besides, I want to play tennis a little longer.

W Well, sure. Why not?

남 음. 나는 오늘 즐거운 시간을 보냈어. 한 번 더 칠래?

여 글쎄. 다른 커플이 이 코트를 사용하고 싶어하는 것 같은데.

남 음. 내 생각에는 저쪽에 있는 저 사람들이 이제 가려고 하는 것 같아. 기다리고 있는 커플은 저 코트를 사용하면 될 것 같은데. 게다가, 나는 테니스를 조금 더 오래 치고 싶어.

여 그래. 물론이지. 왜 안되겠니?

10

① M Can I have a cheeseburger with large fries and a soda?

　 W All right. That will be $5.50, sir.

② M I hope Jennifer can make it to my party Sunday.

　 W Sorry, I'm not going to Jennifer's party.

③ M Lucy, do you know what time it is?

　 W Yeah. It's five minutes till noon.

④ M I can't believe Ms. Cooper is giving us a quiz tomorrow!

　 W Well, I guess we'd better study hard tonight.

⑤ M I saw this really great Chinese movie yesterday.

　 W Really? What's it called?

① 남 치즈 버거 한 개랑, 감자튀김 큰 거 한 개, 그리고 탄산음료 하나 주시겠어요?

　 여 알겠습니다. 5달러 50센트 입니다. 손님.

② 남 Jennifer가 일요일에 내 생일파티에 올 수 있었으면 좋겠어.

　 여 미안하지만, 나는 Jennifer의 파티에 가지 않을거야.

③ 남 Lucy, 지금이 몇 시인지 아니?

　 여 응. 12시 되기 5분 전이야.

④ 남 Cooper 선생님이 내일 퀴즈를 준다니 믿을 수가 없어!

　 여 음. 오늘 밤에 더 열심히 공부를 해야 할 것 같아.

⑤ 남 나 어제 정말 멋진 중국 영화를 봤어.

　 여 정말? 제목이 뭐였는데?

11

W Is there a problem, officer?

여 무슨 문제가 있습니까, 경찰관님?

| M | Yes, ma'am. You're parked in a disabled spot. I'll have to write you a ticket for that. | 남 | 네, 부인. 장애인 전용 공간에 주차를 하셨네요. 딱지를 끊어야 합니다. |

M Yes, ma'am. You're parked in a disabled spot. I'll have to write you a ticket for that.

남 네, 부인. 장애인 전용 공간에 주차를 하셨네요. 딱지를 끊어야 합니다.

W Oh, dear. I had no idea. How much will it be?

여 오, 맙소사. 전 몰랐어요. 얼마인가요?

M It's a $100 ticket.

남 100달러 입니다.

W What? Just for parking in a disabled space? I can't believe it! That's too much!

여 뭐라고요? 장애인 전용 공간에 주차 했다는 이유만으로요? 믿을 수가 없군요! 그건 너무해요!

M Sorry, ma'am. That's the law.

남 죄송합니다, 부인. 그게 법입니다.

12

W Hey, did you get the assignment for science class?

여 있지, 너 과학 수업 숙제 뭔지 아니?

M Yeah. We have to read chapters 1 and 2. Chapter 1 is about forests, and chapter 2 is about deserts.

남 응. 1과랑 2과 읽으면 돼. 1과는 숲에 관한 내용이고, 2과는 사막에 관한 내용이야.

W Okay. Do we have to take the review test, too?

여 알았어. 우리 리뷰테스트도 봐야 하니?

M No, the review test comes after chapter 4. We have to read chapters 3 and 4 first.

남 아니. 리뷰테스트는 4과 다음에 있어. 3과랑 4과 먼저 읽어야 해.

W What are those about?

여 그건 무엇에 관한건데?

M Let's see. Chapter 3 is about rivers, and chapter 4 is about oceans.

남 어디 보자. 3과는 강에 관한 거고, 4과는 바다에 관한 내용이네.

13

M Linda, can you hand me the hammer? I'm trying to put this shelf up.

남 Linda, 망치 좀 건네줄래? 나 이 선반 좀 위에 달으려고.

W Okay. That's kind of high. What are you going to put on it?

여 알았어. 꽤 높아 보이는데. 그 위에 무엇을 올릴 건데?

M Just some old family pictures. Don't worry. We won't have to get anything down from here.

남 오래된 가족 사진들. 걱정하지 마. 여기서 물건을 내려야 할 일은 없을 거야.

W Okay. Just be careful. This ladder is shaking a lot.

여 그래. 조심해. 이 사다리가 많이 흔들려.

14

M Well, Rose, your birthday is coming up. What would you like to do for it?

남 음, Rose, 네 생일이 다가오는구나. 생일날 뭐하고 싶니?

W Dad, I want to have a big dance party with a lot of my friends. Can we please do that?

여 아빠, 저는 여러 친구들과 함께 성대한 댄스파티를 열고 싶어요. 그래도 되나요?

M Uh, not this year. Let's spend time with our family this time. You can have that big

남 흠. 올해에는 하지 말자꾸나. 이번에는 가족들과 함께 시간을 보내자. 내년 열 다섯 번째 생일에 큰 파티를 열면

party for your fifteenth birthday next year.

W Okay, dad.

여   되잖니.

여   알겠어요. 아빠.

15

W Hank? I need help with this formula. I just don't get it.

M Hmm. You don't need to worry about this. It won't be on the test tomorrow.

W Okay. Which formulas will be on the test, then?

M They're all at the end of this chapter. Here, let's go over them one more time.

여   Hank? 이 공식은 네 도움이 필요해. 나는 이것이 이해가 안되거든.

남   흠. 너는 그것을 걱정할 필요가 없어. 그건 내일 시험에 나오지 않거든.

여   알았어. 그럼 어떤 공식들이 시험에 나오는 거야?

남   그것들은 이 과 끝에 나와있어. 여기, 공식들을 한번씩 더 검토해보자.

16

M Mom, have you seen the remote control for the TV?

W Yeah. I left it on the coffee table.

M Uh, no you didn't. I don't see it there.

W Hmm. Maybe I left it on the arm of the chair.

M No, not here, either. Oh, wait. It's over here, right next to the bookshelf.

W That's right!

남   엄마. TV 리모컨 보셨어요?

여   응. 커피 테이블 위에 놔두었어.

남   오. 아니에요. 그곳에 없는걸요.

여   흠. 그럼 의자 팔걸이에 올려놓았나 봐.

남   아니에요. 여기에도 없어요. 오. 잠깐만요. 여기 있네요, 책장 바로 옆에요.

여   그래 맞아!

17

M I've got great news, Sarah! I'm going to visit France next month.

W You're kidding! That's great! But how can you afford it?

M Well, I'm not paying for it. I met my uncle for lunch today, and he said he was going to France on business.

W So you're going with him?

M Yeah. I said that I've always wanted to go. He said that he could get a plane ticket and hotel for me for a low price.

W Wow, that's amazing!

남   나에게 좋은 소식이 있어. Sarah! 나는 다음 달에 프랑스를 방문할 거야.

여   설마! 잘됐다! 그런데 비용은 어떻게 감당하려고?

남   음, 내가 돈을 내지는 않아. 오늘 점심때 삼촌을 만났는데. 그가 프랑스에 출장을 가신대.

여   그래서 그와 함께 가는구나?

남   응. 내가 그곳에 정말 가고 싶었다고 했거든. 그는 나를 위해 비행기 표랑 호텔을 저렴한 가격에 구할 수 있으시대.

여   와우. 그거 멋지구나!

18

M Hey, Rebecca. Can I talk to you for a second?

남   있잖아. Rebecca. 얘기 좀 할 수 있을까?

W Sure. What's up, Dave?

M Well, I was wondering if you were busy Friday night. I've got free movie tickets.

W Oh, sorry. I'm already going out with Kevin.

M Oh, I didn't know that. I'm sorry.

W That's okay.

여 물론이지. 무슨 일이야, Dave?

남 음. 금요일 밤에 시간이 있나 해서. 공짜 영화 표가 생겼거든.

여 오, 미안해. 난 이미 Kevin을 만나기로 했어.

남 오, 몰랐어. 미안해.

여 괜찮아.

19

W Charlie, wake up. You're going to be late for school again.

M Come on, mom. Let me sleep for just five more minutes.

W Oh, no, you don't. You're getting on the bus today. I am absolutely not driving you to school again.

M OK. It won't take me that long to get ready. I won't be late.

여 Charlie, 일어나렴. 학교에 또 지각하겠어.

남 제발요, 엄마. 5분만 더 잘 수 있게 해주세요.

여 오, 그러면 안돼. 오늘은 버스를 타야지. 오늘은 절대 학교까지 태워다 주지 않을 거야.

남 알겠어요. 준비하는데 시간은 얼마 걸리지 않아요. 늦지 않을게요.

20

M Good morning, Miss Parsons. How are you today?

W Fine, Paul. How are you?

M Okay. Actually, I have to talk to you about my presentation next week. I'm afraid I won't be here for it. My family is going to see my aunt and her family in California.

W I see. When will you get back from your trip?

M It should be about two weeks. Can I have the presentation after I come back?

남 좋은 아침이에요, Parsons 선생님. 오늘 기분이 어떠세요?

여 좋단다, Paul. 너는 어떠니?

남 괜찮아요. 사실은요, 다음주에 있을 발표에 대해서 이야기를 좀 하고 싶어요. 저는 발표 때 이곳에 없을 것 같아요. 저희 가족이 캘리포니아에 있는 이모와 그녀의 가족을 보러 가거든요.

여 알겠다. 여행에서 언제 돌아오니?

남 2주 동안 있을 거에요. 돌아와서 발표를 해도 될까요?

모의고사 2회

01 ④	02 ②	03 ④	04 ④	05 ⑤	06 ①	07 ⑤	08 ②	09 ⑤	10 ①
11 ①	12 ④	13 ①	14 ②	15 ③	16 ④	17 ①	18 ④	19 ④	20 ①

01

① M Mom, did you want to see me?

W Yes. I need you to clean the kitchen for me.

② M Can I check out this book?

W Sure. I just need to see your library card, please.

③ M I've never ridden a horse before. It's pretty hard.

W Yeah, at first. But once you learn how, it's fun!

④ M I'll wash the dishes if you dry them.

W That'll work. Make sure you scrub them well, though.

⑤ M Oh! This is one of my favorite shows.

W I don't like this show at all. Let's watch something else.

① 남 엄마, 절 보자고 하셨나요?

여 그래. 나 대신에 부엌 좀 청소하거라.

② 남 이 책을 대여 할 수 있을까요?

여 물론이죠. 도서관 카드만 보여주시면 돼요.

③ 남 난 한 번도 말을 타 본적이 없어. 너무 어려워.

여 맞아, 처음에는. 하지만 일단 방법을 터득하게 되면, 재미있어!

④ 남 네가 물기를 닦는다면 내가 설거지를 할께.

여 그러면 되겠다. 하지만 잘 씻도록 해.

⑤ 남 오! 이건 내가 가장 좋아하는 쇼 중 하나야.

여 나는 이 쇼를 전혀 좋아하지 않아. 우리 다른 거 보자.

02

M Ow! My leg really hurts.

W Sorry to hear that. I hope you didn't injure a muscle or anything.

M Yeah, me too. I don't know why, but this always happens when I run.

W Well, do you stretch before you run?

M No, not really.

W Stretching helps prevent injuries. You should really try that next time.

남 아야! 내 다리가 너무 아파.

여 어떡해. 근육이 다치거나 한건 아니었으면 좋겠어.

남 응. 나도 그래. 왜 그런지 모르겠지만 내가 달리기를 할 때마다 항상 이래.

여 음, 너 달리기 하기 전에 스트레칭 하니?

남 아니. 안 해.

여 스트레칭은 부상을 예방하게 하지. 다음 번에는 스트레칭을 하도록 해.

03

W Excuse me, I'm ready to order my food now.

M All right. ma'am. What would you like?

여 여기요. 이제 주문할게요.

남 알겠습니다. 부인. 어떤 것으로 하시겠습니까?

W	I'd like this vegetable pasta, please. Can I also have your soup of the day?	여	저는 이 야채 파스타로 할게요. 오늘의 수프도 주시겠어요?
M	Yes, ma'am. It's broccoli soup.	남	네. 부인. 브로컬리 수프에요.
W	That's fine. Also, I'd like some iced tea to drink, please.	여	알겠습니다. 그리고. 아이스 티 한잔도 부탁 드려요.
M	Okay. Will there be anything else?	남	네. 더 필요하신 것이 있으신가요?
W	Yes. Could you get me another glass of water, please? This glass looks dirty.	여	네. 물 한잔 더 주시겠어요? 이 잔은 지저분해보여요.
M	Certainly, ma'am.	남	물론입니다. 부인.

04

| M | Today the President said that he would help victims of the recent deadly storms. The President said he would send in soldiers and doctors to help these victims. Over a hundred people have died because of these terrible storms. Many small towns across the country have been destroyed, and millions have no electricity or water. | 남 | 대통령은 오늘 최근의 극심한 폭풍우로 인한 피해자들에게 도움을 줄 것이라고 했습니다. 대통령은 이러한 피해자들을 돕기 위해 군인들과 의사들을 보낼 것이라고 했습니다. 100명이 넘는 사람들이 이번의 심한 폭풍우로 인하여 사망했습니다. 전국의 여러 작은 도시들은 파괴 되었으며, 수백 명의 사람들은 전기와 물 공급을 받지 못하고 있습니다. |

05

W	All right! I love this song.	여	좋았어! 난 이 노래가 좋아!
M	Hey, sis, your stereo is a little loud. Do you think you could turn it down?	남	있지. 누나. 오디오 소리가 좀 큰 것 같아. 소리 좀 줄여 줄래?
W	But listening to music helps me study! And I have a lot of homework to do tonight.	여	하지만 난 음악을 들으면 공부하는데 도움이 된단 말이야! 그리고 나는 오늘 밤에 해야 할 숙제가 굉장히 많아.
M	Maybe so, but it makes it harder for me to study. And I have a lot of homework to do, too.	남	그럴수도 있어. 하지만 난 더 공부하기가 힘들단 말이야. 그리고 나도 해야 할 숙제가 많아.
W	Okay, fine. I guess I can listen through my headphones.	여	그래. 알았어. 헤드폰으로 들어야겠다.

06

M	Hey, honey. Are you done with band practice now?	남	얘야. 밴드 연습이 이제서야 끝난 거니?
W	Yeah, we had to stay a little late today. We've got a big performance in two weeks.	여	네. 오늘은 좀 더 늦게까지 있어야 했어요. 2주 뒤에 중요한 공연이 있거든요.
M	Oh, really? I look forward to seeing it. By the way, we have to stop by the store real quickly. I need to pick up some milk and a	남	오 그러니? 나도 보고 싶구나. 그건 그렇고. 가게 좀 빨리 들러야겠구나. 우유와 다른 몇 가지를 사가야 해.

few other things.

W That's fine. I don't have much homework to do tonight.

여 알겠어요. 오늘 저녁엔 해야 할 숙제가 많이 없거든요.

07

① W I'm so tired! I worked so hard today.

M You should relax and watch some TV, then.

② W I just got a letter from my brother today.

M That's cool. How's he doing?

③ W Hey, what's wrong with your dog?

M She's been a little sick lately.

④ W My mom and dad just celebrated 30 years of marriage.

M That's nice. They must be really happy together.

⑤ W Would you like any more chicken?

M That was an excellent steak, Mom.

① 여 너무 피곤해! 오늘은 정말 열심히 일했어.

남 그럼 휴식을 취하면서 TV 시청을 좀 해.

② 여 나는 오늘 남동생에게 편지를 받았어.

남 잘됐네. 그는 어떻게 지내니?

③ 여 이봐. 네 강아지 왜 그래?

남 그녀는 최근 몸이 좀 안 좋아.

④ 여 우리 엄마 아빠가 결혼 30주년을 기념하셨어.

남 잘됐네. 그분들은 정말로 행복하실 거야.

⑤ 여 치킨 좀 더 먹을래?

남 정말 훌륭한 스테이크였어요. 엄마.

08

W Hey, Steve. You must have had a pretty bad morning, huh?

M You're not kidding! It's all this heavy rain outside. My umbrella couldn't keep me dry at all.

W I know. Traffic was really slow because of it.

M Yeah. I just hope it will be sunny tomorrow.

여 이봐. Steve. 오늘은 일진이 안 좋은 날이었겠네.

남 말도 마! 밖에 진짜 비가 많이 와. 우산을 써도 다 젖었다니까.

여 알아. 그래서 교통정체도 심했잖아.

남 맞아. 내일은 맑았으면 좋겠어.

09

W Where are you going, Pete?

M I'm going to visit Larry. Don't worry. I'll be back in a few hours.

W All right. Are you going to take the car, then?

M No, I don't have to. Larry lives just a few blocks down the street. Besides, I've wanted to go bike riding for a while.

여 어디 가. Pete?

남 Larry 만나러 가. 걱정하지 마. 몇 시간 내로 돌아올 거야.

여 알겠어. 그럼 차 가지고 가는 거니?

남 아니. 그럴 필요 없어. Larry는 그저 몇 블록 아래에 살고 있거든. 게다가, 나는 한동안 자전거를 타고 싶었었거든.

10

W Yesterday I was out hiking with my friend Debbie. We were in the beautiful woods, and we saw a lot of birds and squirrels. It was a really nice day. But Debbie suddenly fell into a small pool of mud. Her clothes got dirty and she hurt her ankle. Thankfully, these two guys came along and helped us. They carried Debbie out of the woods, and we went to a doctor right away. Debbie will be fine, but she doesn't want to hike for a while.

여 어제 나는 내 친구인 Debbie와 하이킹을 했다. 우리는 아름다운 숲 속에 있었는데. 많은 새들과 다람쥐들을 보았습니다. 굉장히 화창한 날이었습니다. 하지만 Debbie가 갑자기 작은 진흙탕에 빠졌습니다. 그녀의 옷은 더러워졌고, 그녀는 발목에 부상을 입었습니다. 고맙게도, 두 명의 청년들이 다가와 우리를 도와주었습니다. 그들은 Debbie를 숲 밖으로 데리고 나와주었고, 우리는 바로 의사에게로 갔습니다. Debbie는 괜찮아질 것이지만. 한동안은 하이킹을 하고 싶어하지 않습니다.

11

W So, Mark, where do you usually spend your pocket money?

M I buy comic books with most of it.

W Really? What kind of comics do you like?

M Well, I like superhero comics. But there are other types, like horror, mysteries, and dramas. I like a lot of different ones. What about you?

W Well, I love to collect my favorite singers' new albums. I really enjoy listening to them whenever I have free time.

여 그래서. Mark. 너는 주로 용돈을 어디에 사용하니?

남 나는 대부분 만화책을 사.

여 정말? 너는 어떤 종류의 만화책을 좋아하니?

남 음. 나는 슈퍼히어로 만화책을 좋아해. 하지만 공포. 미스터리, 드라마와 같은 다른 종류도 있어. 너는?

여 음. 나는 내가 좋아하는 가수들의 새로운 앨범들을 수집하는 걸 좋아해. 나는 시간이 날 때마다 그 앨범들을 감상하는 것을 굉장히 즐겨.

12

W So what did you do this weekend?

M I went to a *Star Wars* exhibition.

W Cool. So what did you do there?

M Well, I watched some of the *Star Wars* films there. I also went to lots of talks about the movies, and some included interviews with the stars. Oh, and a lot of people dressed up like the movies' characters!

W Did you dress up?

M No, I didn't. But I did buy a lot of books and toys for my collection, though.

여 그래서 너는 주말에 무엇을 했니?

남 나는 「스타워즈」 전시회에 다녀왔어.

여 멋지다. 너는 그곳에서 무엇을 했니?

남 음. 나는 그곳에서 「스타워즈」 영화를 몇 편 보았어. 나는 영화와 관련된 강연에도 여러 군데 갔었는데. 영화배우들과 인터뷰를 하는 곳도 있었어. 오. 그리고 많은 사람들이 영화의 캐릭터처럼 옷을 입었더라고!

여 너도 복장을 입었니?

남 아니. 하지만 나는 내 수집품을 위한 책과 장난감을 많이 샀어.

13

W Merry Christmas, Billy! I hope you like this present.

여 메리 크리스마스, Billy! 네가 이 선물을 좋아했으면 좋겠어.

M Wow! It's that video game I wanted. Thanks, Mom!	남 와우! 이거 제가 원하던 비디오 게임이네요. 감사해요, 엄마!
W You're welcome, dear.	여 아니란다. 얘야.
M But you know... I'm sorry I couldn't get you anything.	남 하지만 있잖아요. 죄송하지만 저는 아무것도 준비를 못 했어요.
W That's OK. I'm happy just seeing you enjoy your presents.	여 괜찮다. 나는 네가 선물을 받고 기뻐하는 모습을 보는 것만으로도 기쁘단다.

14

M Excuse me.	남 실례합니다.
W Yes, sir. How can I help you?	여 네, 손님. 무엇을 도와드릴까요?
M Why haven't we left the airport yet? Our flight was supposed to leave at 9:30. It's almost 10:00 o'clock now.	남 왜 아직 비행기가 이륙을 안 하는 거죠? 우리 비행기는 9시 30분에 이륙하기로 되어 있었잖아요. 지금 10시가 다 되어가잖아요.
W We're sorry for that, sir. Some flights had to land suddenly. We'll have to wait for them to clear out.	여 죄송합니다. 손님. 일부 비행기들이 갑자기 착륙을 해야 했습니다. 저희는 착륙이 완료될 때까지 기다려야 합니다.
M I was hoping we'd take off as soon as possible.	남 되도록이면 빨리 출발했으면 싶어서요.
W Well, it shouldn't be too much longer.	여 음. 그리 오래 걸리진 않을 겁니다.

15

W This is a thing people use all the time. In fact, people use it all the time in school. You need this for math and science classes. You can use this to add and subtract numbers. In fact, you can solve all kinds of math problems with this. That's all you can do with this device, though.	여 이것은 사람들이 늘 사용하는 것이다. 사실, 사람들은 이것을 학교에서 항상 사용한다. 여러분은 수학과 과학 수업 때문에 이것이 필요하다. 여러분은 이것을 숫자를 더하고 뺄 때 사용한다. 사실상. 여러분은 모든 수학 문제를 이것을 사용하여 풀 수 있다. 하지만 그것이 여러분이 이것을 사용하여 할 수 있는 전부이다.

16

M Hey, Carol.	남 어이. Carol.
W Steve, you look different. Say, did you get a haircut?	여 Steve. 너 달라 보이네. 머리 자른 거야?
M Yeah. I wanted to try something new. So what do you think?	남 응. 나는 색다른걸 시도해보고 싶었거든. 어떤 것 같아?
W Well, I think you definitely look much younger with it. But I liked your old haircut.	여 음. 그 머리를 하니 확실히 훨씬 더 어려 보이네. 하지만 나는 너의 예전 헤어 스타일이 좋았어.
M I thought my old haircut was too strange, though. I wanted something stylish.	남 하지만 나는 내 예전 헤어 스타일이 이상한 것 같았거든. 나는 좀 더 세련된 머리를 하고 싶었어.

17

W   Ugh. I really don't feel like taking a test today.

M   Why? What's the matter?

W   I was up all night last night. I just couldn't get any sleep.

M   Oh. Were you studying?

W   No. I know all the stuff for the test already. I was just watching a lot of movies on TV. Now I'm just trying to keep my eyes open.

M   Well, you shouldn't have done that. You can't focus on your test without enough sleep.

여   어. 난 오늘 정말 시험을 칠 기분이 아니야.

남   왜? 무슨 문제 있어?

여   어제 밤을 샜거든. 잠을 한 숨도 못 잤어.

남   오. 공부한 거야?

여   아니. 시험에 나올 사항들은 이미 다 알고 있어. 단지 TV에서 방영해주는 여러 영화들을 시청했어. 지금은 눈을 뜨고 있으려고 노력 중이야.

남   음. 너는 그러지 말았어야 했어. 충분한 잠을 자지 않고서는 시험에 집중을 할 수가 없단 말이야.

18

M   Lacy, are you going to the Dogwood Festival next month?

W   Uh, that depends. When does it begin?

M   It starts on Monday, June 7th.

W   Hmm. Well, I'll be out of town until Thursday, June 10th. When does it end?

M   Saturday, June 12th.

W   Ah. I have to work that day. Let's go there the day before that.

M   Sure.

남   Lacy, 너 다음 달에 Dogwood 축제에 가니?

여   어, 봐서. 언제 시작하는데?

남   6월 7일 월요일에 시작해.

여   흠. 나는 6월 10일 목요일까지 도시에 없을 거야. 축제가 언제 끝나는데?

남   6월 12일 토요일에.

여   아. 나 그 날은 일해야 되는데. 그 전날에 가자.

남   그래.

19

M   Are you studying a foreign language this year?

W   Yes. I've started studying Japanese.

M   Japanese, huh? How is that going for you?

W   Well, it's very different from English. So I have to learn a lot of new rules for forming sentences. Not only that, but I have to learn two new alphabets and hundreds of new symbols, too!

남   너 올해 외국어 공부하는 거니?

여   응. 나 일본어 배우기 시작했어.

남   일본어라고? 잘 되어가고 있니?

여   음. 영어랑은 굉장히 달라. 그래서 문장을 구성하는 새로운 규칙들을 많이 공부해야 해. 그 뿐만이 아니라, 두 개의 새로운 알파벳과 수백 개의 새로운 기호들도 배워야 한다고!

20

W   Last week I visited a farm. It was very

여   지난 주에. 나는 농장을 방문했습니다. 굉장히 흥미로웠

interesting, but it was also kind of sad. I felt bad as I looked at all the cows, pigs, and chickens. That's because I knew they were all going to be killed and turned into food. This made me feel really bad. I mean, what if they were my pets?

지만 나는 슬프기도 했습니다. 나는 소와 돼지 그리고 닭을 바라보면서 기분이 좋지 않았습니다. 왜냐하면 그들이 도살을 당해 음식이 될 것을 알고 있었기 때문입니다. 이것은 내 기분을 상당히 나쁘게 했습니다. 내 말은, 그들이 내 애완 동물이었더라면 어떻게 했겠어요?

모의고사 3회

01 ④	02 ⑤	03 ④	04 ④	05 ⑤	06 ②	07 ④	08 ③	09 ⑤	10 ⑤
11 ④	12 ③	13 ②	14 ③	15 ⑤	16 ①	17 ④	18 ①	19 ③	20 ⑤

01

M ① A man and a woman are dancing together.
② A boy and a girl are playing with toys.
③ A woman is reading a book.
④ A boy is surfing at the beach.
⑤ A man is playing the violin.

남 ① 남자와 여자는 함께 춤을 추고 있다.
② 소년과 소녀는 장난감을 가지고 놀고 있다.
③ 여자는 책을 읽고 있다.
④ 소년은 해변에서 서핑을 하고 있다.
⑤ 남자는 바이올린을 켜고 있다.

02

M Paula, I need to talk with you about something.
W What's up?
M It's about Mom's birthday. I'm going to get her this coat she wants. What are you going to get her?
W I'm not sure. I don't know what she wants.
M Well, Dad said she would like a new TV for her bedroom. You could help him pay for one.
W That might work. I'll talk to Dad about it.

남 Paula, 너와 얘기를 좀 하고 싶어.
여 뭔데?
남 엄마의 생신에 관한 얘기야. 난 그녀가 원하는 이 코트를 사 드릴 거야. 너는 무엇을 사드릴 거니?
여 잘 모르겠어. 난 그녀가 무엇을 원하시는지 모르겠어.
남 음, 아빠가 그러셨는데 그녀는 침실에 놓을 새로운 TV를 가지고 싶어하신대. 그가 그것을 사실 수 있게 돈을 보태면 될 것 같아.
여 그러면 되겠다. 그것에 관해 아빠와 이야기를 해 봐야겠어.

03

W All right, class. We're going to do a little science activity right now. You'll have to get into pairs for this. Now, who's missing today?
M Jake, Louis, Mary, and Milton.
W So four people are missing, huh? That means you'll have to get into 13 pairs. Everyone find a partner now.
M Yes, ma'am.

여 좋아요, 여러분. 우리는 지금 과학활동을 좀 해보려고 합니다. 이것을 하기 위해 여러분은 두 명씩 짝을 지어 주시기 바랍니다. 자, 오늘은 누가 결석을 했죠?
남 Jake, Louis, Mary 그리고 Milton이요.
여 그럼 네 명이 결석을 한 것이군요, 그렇죠? 그렇다면 13쌍을 만들면 되겠네요. 자, 모두 자신의 파트너를 찾으세요.
남 네, 선생님.

04

M Hey, Barbara. A couple of us are going out to eat after work. You want to come along?

W That depends. Where are you all going?

M There's this new seafood restaurant over in Southport. We thought we might give it a try.

W Oh. Sorry, but I think I'll pass. I don't want to go all the way up there.

M Oh, okay. Maybe some other time, then.

W Maybe. Thanks anyway, though.

남 저기, Barbara. 우리 두 사람은 퇴근 후에 외식 할 거야. 너도 같이 갈래?

여 봐서. 어디로 가는데?

남 Southport에 새로 생긴 해산물 식당이 있어. 거기에서 먹어볼까 했지.

여 오. 미안하지만 안 갈래. 그렇게 먼 길을 가고 싶지는 않아.

남 오. 알겠어. 그럼 다음에 가자.

여 그러던지. 어쨌든 고마워.

05

W Well, I just got done sweeping the kitchen and bathroom.

M That's good. I'm almost done dusting the furniture. So what does that leave?

W Hmm. Well, we've already put all the books back on the shelves. And we've already washed all the dishes.

M Really? I think that's all.

여 음. 나 방금 부엌이랑 욕실 청소 끝냈어.

남 좋았어. 난 가구에 있는 먼지털기를 거의 다 했어. 남아 있는 일이 뭐지?

여 흠. 우리는 이미 책장에 책을 도로 다 꽂았어. 그리고 설거지도 다 끝냈어.

남 그래? 그럼 다 한 것 같아.

06

M ① Stone City had its highest summer temperatures in 2007.

② Stone City's average summer temperature was the same in 2006 and 2008.

③ Stone City had its lowest summer temperature in 2005.

④ Stone City's average summer temperature in 2010 was lower than that of 2006.

⑤ Stone City's average summer temperature in 2009 was higher than that of 2008.

남 ① Stone 도시는 2007년에 가장 높은 여름철 기온을 기록했다.

② Stone 도시의 평균 여름철 기온은 2006년과 2008년에 동일했다.

③ Stone 도시는 2005년에 가장 낮은 여름철 기온을 기록했다.

④ 2010년의 Stone 도시의 평균 여름철 기온은 2006년보다 낮았다.

⑤ 2009년의 Stone 도시의 평균 여름철 기온은 2008년보다 높았다.

07

W Do you see it?

M No. Are you sure you dropped your earring under here?

여 보여?

남 아니. 여기에 귀걸이 떨어뜨린 게 확실해?

W Yes. I saw it roll on the floor and go under the bed.

M Well, I'm down on my knees looking and reaching under here. But I don't see it. Maybe it's under that rug.

W Maybe. Would you check and see?

M Okay. Yeah, here it is.

여 응. 바닥에 구르면서 침대 밑으로 들어가는걸 봤어.

남 음. 무릎 꿇고 아래쪽을 찾아보고 있어. 그런데 보이지가 않아. 저 매트 아래 있을 수도 있어.

여 그럴지도. 네가 확인 좀 해줄래?

남 알겠어. 그래. 여기 있네.

08

M Uh-oh. I just realized that I don't have any cash on me.

W Is that a problem?

M Uh, yeah. I had to park in a parking lot. I have to pay for my time there, but they only take cash.

W Oh. What are you going to do?

M Well, would you help me out? I just need $10. I promise I'll pay you back.

W Well, okay.

남 어. 나에게 현금이 한 푼도 없다는 게 방금 생각났어.

여 그게 문제가 돼?

남 응. 나 주차장에 주차해야 했거든. 주차한 시간만큼 금액을 지불해야 하는데, 현금만 받거든.

여 오. 어떻게 하려고?

남 음. 나에게 도움을 줄래? 10달러만 있으면 돼. 반드시 갚을게.

여 음. 알겠어.

09

M Excuse me, but could you help me with something?

W Sure. What is it?

M I need to get a new cord for my television.

W Well, the best kind is an HDMI cable. It looks like this.

M Uh. I don't think that will work with my TV.

W Oh, then this should. It's called component video, and it has a red, blue, and green plug. This will give you a really good picture, too.

M Great! I'll buy it then.

남 실례하지만, 저 좀 도와주시겠어요?

여 물론이죠. 왜 그러시죠?

남 제 TV에 연결할 새로운 선을 사려고 해요.

여 음, 가장 좋은 것은 HDMI 케이블 입니다. 이렇게 생긴 것이죠.

남 어. 이건 제 TV에 맞지 않을 것 같아요.

여 오, 그럼 이건 맞을 거에요. 이건 컴포넌트 비디오라고 불리는 것인데요, 빨강. 파랑. 초록색 플러그가 있어요. 최상의 화질도 전달해 주지요.

남 좋군요. 그걸로 살게요.

10

W Hi, my name is Tracy Bolton. It's nice to meet you all. I just moved here from Los Angeles, and I'm in the eighth grade. I've joined this speech club because I want to become a lawyer someday. I hope my time here will help me improve my public speaking skills. Thanks.

여 안녕하세요. 제 이름은 Tracy Bolton이에요. 여러분을 만나게 되어 반가워요. 저는 로스 앤젤레스에서 이곳으로 이사를 왔고, 8학년 이에요. 저는 언젠간 변호사가 되고 싶어서 이 웅변 동아리에 가입을 했어요. 저는 이곳에서의 시간이 저의 웅변 실력을 향상시켜줄 것이라고 생각해요. 고맙습니다.

11

W Okay, Dave. I have to do some shopping for dresses and shoes. What do you want to do?

M I think I'm going to look at some comic books over at the bookstore, Mom.

W That's fine. Let's meet at Welk's Department Store in half an hour.

M Okay. Where exactly should we meet?

W Hmm. Do you know where the restrooms are in that store?

M Yeah.

W From there, walk towards the men's department. Walk past that department and turn left towards the cashier counter. I'll meet you there.

여 좋아, Dave. 나는 드레스와 신발을 쇼핑할거야. 너는 무엇을 하고 싶니?

남 저는 서점에 가서 만화책을 보려고요, 엄마.

여 알겠다. 그럼 30분 뒤에 Welk's 백화점에서 보자꾸나.

남 알겠어요. 정확히 어디에서 만나죠?

여 흠. 백화점 안에 화장실이 어디에 있는지 아니?

남 네.

여 그곳에서, 남성복 매장으로 걸어와. 그 매장을 지나고 좌회전을 해서 계산대까지 쭉 걸어오거라. 그곳에서 만나자.

12

M Good morning, everyone. This is your pilot speaking. This flight is heading to Hong Kong, and it will be a 7-hour trip. Please shut off any cell phones, computers, or other electronic devices now. Also, please fasten your seat belts. Do not unfasten them until you see the sign. Thank you for flying Alpha Airlines.

남 좋은 아침입니다, 여러분. 저는 여러분을 모시고 가는 기장입니다. 이것은 홍콩으로 가는 항공편이며, 도착하는데 7시간이 걸릴 것입니다. 휴대전화나 컴퓨터, 또는 다른 전자기기의 전원을 지금 꺼주시기 바랍니다. 또한, 안전벨트를 착용해주시기 바랍니다. 사인이 켜질 때까지 안전벨트를 풀지 말아 주십시오. 저희 Alpha 항공을 이용해 주셔서 감사합니다.

13

W Charlie, what's wrong?

M The Patriots lost the football game last night. I was really hoping that they would win.

W Well, that's not too bad. I mean, it was just one game.

M No, it wasn't. Now they can't play for the championship. I'm just – I can't believe it. It doesn't seem real at all.

여 Charlie, 무슨 일 있어?

남 어제 밤에 Patriots가 미식축구 경기에서 패했어. 난 정말 그들이 이기길 바랬는데.

여 음, 그리 나쁘진 않은데. 내 말은, 그저 경기일 뿐이잖아.

남 아니야. 이제 그들은 결승전에 진출을 못한단 말이야. 난 단지 믿을 수가 없어. 사실일리가 없어.

14

W Who can solve this problem? Can you do it, Ralph?

M Let's see. Is it 100, Ms. Walker?

여 이 문제 누가 풀어보겠니? 네가 할 수 있겠니, Ralph?

남 어디 보자. 100인가요, Walker 선생님?

W No, I'm afraid that's incorrect. The answer is 169.

M Ah. I'm sorry. I didn't memorize the formulas yet.

W Well, you need to study them harder. These are going to be on the next test.

여 안됐지만 오답이란다. 정답은 169야.

남 아. 죄송해요. 제가 아직 공식을 못 외웠어요.

여 음. 넌 더 열심히 공부를 해야겠구나. 이것들은 다음 시험에 나올 거야.

15

M Well, it looks like we've got fleas in our house.

W Are you serious? How did you get fleas in your house?

M I'm almost certain they're from our dog. He goes outside sometimes. And I think he picked some fleas up there.

W Oh, I guess you'll have to hire someone to kill them.

남 음. 우리 집에 벼룩이 있는 것 같아.

여 정말이야? 어떻게 하다 집에 벼룩이 생겼어?

남 분명히 우리 집 개 때문이야. 그는 때때로 밖으로 나가거든. 난 그가 벼룩을 밖에서 옮아왔다고 생각해.

여 오. 사람을 불러서 벼룩을 죽여야 할 것 같아.

16

W Paxton Elementary is currently looking for a bright and hard-working teacher. This person will teach English and math to students in the third, fourth, and fifth grades. This is a full-time position, and it will pay $40,000 a year. You must have a degree from a respected college. For more info, call Dr. Ross at 777-9045.

여 Paxton 초등학교는 현재 능력 있고 열정 있는 선생님을 찾고 있습니다. 3학년, 4학년, 그리고 5학년 학생들에게 영어와 수학을 가르치게 될 것입니다. 전임이며, 연봉은 40,000달러입니다. 반드시 명문대학의 학사 학위를 소지하고 계셔야 합니다. 더 많은 정보를 알고 싶으시면, Ross 박사님에게 777-9045번으로 전화 주시기 바랍니다.

17

M You look pretty upset. Is something the matter?

W Uh-huh. This is the worst day of my life!

M Why do you say that?

W My boyfriend broke up with me today.

M Oh. I'm really sorry to hear that, Cassie.

W I thought he really liked me, too! I just don't understand what happened.

M Cheer up. It hurts now, but in time you'll feel better.

남 화가 나 보이네. 무슨 문제 있어?

여 응. 내 생에서 최악의 날이야!

남 왜 그러는 거야?

여 오늘 내 남자친구가 헤어지자고 했어.

남 오. 안됐구나. Cassie.

여 나는 그도 나를 정말 좋아한다고 생각했어! 무슨 일이 일어난 건지 모르겠어.

남 기운 내. 지금은 아프겠지만, 곧 괜찮아질 거야.

18

M Good morning, Jessica. What would you

남 좋은 아침이야. Jessica. 아침으로 무엇을 먹고 싶니?

like for breakfast?

W I'm not sure. Are you cooking something?

M Just some toast, eggs, and bacon.

W Well, to be honest, I'm not really that hungry. I guess I'll have some toast, though.

M Want any juice to drink?

W Uh, no thanks.

여 잘 모르겠어. 너 요리하고 있는 거니?

남 토스트랑 계란 그리고 베이컨이야.

여 음. 실은. 난 별로 배가 고프지 않아. 난 그냥 토스트 좀 먹을래.

남 주스도 좀 마실래?

여 아니. 괜찮아.

19

M Before I start today's lesson, I want to talk about our class trip this Friday. I think our trip to the museum is going to be very fun. However, I see that many of you haven't turned in the permission forms yet. Remember, your parents must sign these forms, or else you can't go. There are only three days left before the trip.

남 오늘 수업을 시작하기 전에, 저는 이번 주 금요일에 있을 수학여행에 대해 얘기를 하고 싶군요. 박물관으로의 수학여행은 굉장히 재미 있을 것입니다. 하지만, 저는 여러분들 중 상당수가 아직도 허가서를 제출하지 않았다는 것을 알고 있습니다. 기억하세요. 여러분의 부모님이 이 허가서에 사인을 해야만 합니다. 그렇지 않으면 여러분은 갈 수 없어요. 수학여행을 가기까지 3일밖에 남지 않았습니다.

20

W Hey, Michael. What's up?

M Hey. I'm looking to see if there are any light meals on this menu. I'm trying to lose some weight.

W Really? I was on a special diet not too long ago, too. I actually lost 15 pounds in just a few weeks!

M I don't believe it! What's your secret?

W Well, I drank water with all my meals. That actually made me less hungry, so I ate less.

여 이봐. Michael. 무슨 일이야?

남 응. 난 이 메뉴에서 간단한 식사가 있을까 하고 보고 있는 중이었어. 몸무게를 감량하려고 하고 있거든.

여 정말이니? 나도 얼마 전에 특별한 다이어트를 했었어. 나 사실 단 몇 주 만에 15파운드를 감량했어!

남 믿기지가 않아! 비결이 뭐야?

여 음. 나는 식사를 할 때마다 물을 마셨어. 그럼 나는 덜 배가 고파지고, 덜 먹게 되는 거지.

센치한 Listening 길들이기

중학 영어 내신 만점을 향한 길들이기 시리즈

- 센치한 Listening 길들이기 총 6권
- 도도한 Reading 길들이기 총 6권
- 까칠한 Grammar 길들이기 총 6권

www.compasspub.com/LG